INTRODUCTION

Some of my most enjoyable times have been teaching, especially on subjects pertaining to religion. A significant venue where this took place was in a Sunday school class my wife and I attended for years. I liked it when people agreed with my point of view. I have to admit I was disappointed if I didn't get some disagreement about what I was presenting. There were those in the class who considered me to be a radical. There were even those who made efforts to keep me from teaching. I considered that as just something which goes with the territory. One of the greatest compliments to my teaching was the comment of a class member when she was informed I would be teaching: "Oh no, we have to think again." Success in teaching for me was not gaining agreement from all class members. Success was getting class members to think through why they believed what they did. Much of what I write comes from outlines of these Sunday school classes taught over the years since I retired from the Army. It has been a great journey, and it has not ended, but continues down a pathway filled with new growth at every intersection.

My greatest concern about putting down my thoughts is that some will try to use it as an excuse to reject Christianity. They will see my words as a reason to do so. That is something most distant from my thinking. I write these words for those who discount the message of the Bible because they see it as not being historical, scientific, or literal, so of little value. They have never been taught that, metaphorically and symbolically, it carries great truth. I write it for those whose hearts cannot accept what their minds cannot believe. My hope is readers will be able to grasp the truth of the Bible that lies within the myth and metaphor found on the pages of scripture. I hope they will also come to realize that questions can lead to growth, and you don't need to have an answer for everything.

So here is a word of caution: If you are reading this to find arguments discounting Christianity, read no further. I reiterate: this is not written to discount Christianity. It is written to discuss what I believe to be some of the erroneous views surrounding what it means to be Christian and how scripture is to be interpreted. To question certain held beliefs and the history of parts of the Bible is by no means meant to discount the truths of the Bible.

The reality is, two of the groups of people I would most like to reach are the ones who most likely will not read what I write. The first group encompasses those individuals who will be concerned their preconceived ideas about Christianity and the Bible—in which they don't believe—would be questioned. The second group has a similar attitude but a different touch. This group encompasses those who are afraid their preconceived ideas about Christianity and the Bible—in which they do believe—would be questioned. The fear of individuals in both these groups is they would have to reevaluate their belief systems. This is a scary undertaking if you are convinced you are right about what you believe or don't believe. It could actually lead to a transformation of the way you live. But, isn't that the true meaning of the ministry of Jesus? One who transforms? There is a third group I have as a target: those practicing Christians who have no idea how to respond to the two groups listed above. Hopefully what I have written will give them some ammunition to say, "The way you see it is not necessarily the way it is." In actuality, none of us see things as they are; we see things as we are. We see things as where we were when. The fourth and last group I have in mind I refer to as the "seekers." Seekers are those who believe

GOD IN A BOX:

*Thoughts from a
Recovering Fundamentalist*

MARION PEMBER

The opinions expressed in this manuscript are solely the opinions of the author and do not represent the opinions or thoughts of the publisher. The author has represented and warranted full ownership and/or legal right to publish all the materials in this book.

God in a Box:
Thoughts from a Recovering Fundamentalist
All Rights Reserved.
Copyright © 2014 Marion Pember
v4.0

Cover Photo © 2014 JupiterImages Corporation. All rights reserved - used with permission.

This book may not be reproduced, transmitted, or stored in whole or in part by any means, including graphic, electronic, or mechanical without the express written consent of the publisher except in the case of brief quotations embodied in critical articles and reviews.

Outskirts Press, Inc.
http://www.outskirtspress.com

ISBN: 978-1-4787-0204-7

Outskirts Press and the "OP" logo are trademarks belonging to Outskirts Press, Inc.

PRINTED IN THE UNITED STATES OF AMERICA

The Scripture quotations contained herein are from the New Revised Standard Version Bible, copyright 1989 by the Division of Christian Education of the National Council of the Churches of Christ in the U.S.A. Used by permission. All rights reserved.

CONTENTS

INTRODUCTION..vii
HOW IT ALL BEGAN 1
THE BIBLE: WORD OF GOD OR GOD'S WORDS?................10
I BELIEVE IN GOD: WHAT DOES IT MEAN? 39
WHO IS JESUS? 67
MIRACLES: WHAT, WHY, AND HOW?................................101
THE HEREAFTER: HEAVEN, HELL, PURGATORY OR…?...126
RELIGION: HOW? WHY? 146
CONCLUSION 168
BIBLIOGRAPHY..170

there is something to the Christian faith, but have trouble with some of the dogma, and are unable to accept all that they hear. Maybe this will give them a different way to look and listen.

That leads me to a statement expressing where I am concerning the Christian message. I borrow this from an article by Bishop John Shelby Spong in which he tells the story of Harrisena Community Church in Lake George, New York. On the back of their Sunday bulletins is printed the following:

"We believe in the profound message brought to humankind by Jesus of Nazareth. We believe that it is in this message rather than the institutions conveying it that forms the most enduring foundation for a positive life. We believe that Christ's message is at least as germane to the world today as it was two thousand years ago. We believe that this message better enables each of us to see and worship God in our own way. We believe that Christianity is enriched by human reason not in conflict with it. We believe that as a church family, we are responsible to one another and our community."

I do not claim to be a scholar. I do claim to be one who reads widely and processes what I read through my own rational radar screen. I am unable to identify the exact source of all that I have read, heard, and studied, which has brought me to a particular stance on any issue. There are times throughout the text when I refer to fundamentalists' beliefs or interpretations. I am well aware some Christians who consider themselves to not be fundamentalist or even conservative will say, "That's what I believe, and I'm not a fundamentalist." I am also aware there are conservative Christians who hold some of the same beliefs I attribute to fundamentalists. I don't believe a conservative Christian would hold to all the beliefs I attribute to fundamentalists. If you call yourself a conservative Christian and do hold to all that I attribute to fundamentalists, then—let us be honest—you probably are a fundamentalist!

In the chapters that follow I make no attempt to cover the spectrum of Christian beliefs. I have chosen several I have observed to be of greatest interest to Christians I know. You will also note I raise questions for which I give no answers. This is somewhat intentional because one of my goals is to get the readers to take a look at what is in their God box. Another reason is simply because for some questions I raise there are no answers. Some issues may go in different directions than you have ever traveled. That also is intentional, and another attempt to challenge you to think about what you have in your God box. My theory is that questions create growth. I hope what I have written becomes a stimulant for growth.

One final note concerning any quoted scripture. Unless otherwise stated I will be using the New Revised Standard Version (NRSV).

1
HOW IT ALL BEGAN

Box: A container, usually rectangular or square, with four sides, a bottom, and a lid. The lid can be very important to keep the contents in place. Sometimes boxes and their contents are stored and forgotten. Years later they are discovered in musty basements or hot attic spaces. When opened and viewed, the contents are sometimes surprising to the viewer who initially stored the box.

God: That to which some refer as their higher power. What does God have to do with boxes? But wait, I am getting ahead of myself. I need to start at the beginning.

How do you begin writing about where your own journey of faith began and about your present beliefs? How can you explain all the nuances and experiences that influenced you? How is it possible to give credit to all those in your past who have helped you reach the place where you are, both those with whom you agreed, and those with whom you disagreed? How can you explain the struggles over issues of faith that have shaped you? You probably can't explain everything, but in telling your story you can try. That is the task I have undertaken.

As already stated, I read a lot and assimilate some of what I read into my own thought patterns. To become assimilated in my own belief system, an idea has to pass the test of rationality. I can't assimilate something into my belief system "just because." A concept that runs counter to scholarly research cannot be accepted on "blind faith." Please do not interpret this to mean faith has no place in the scheme of things. It is also important for me to explain why I even want to do this. Three things stand out in my mind. The first is encouragement received from friends, many who sat patiently and listened to me talk about what was inside my God box and suggested I should write a book.

The second was a strong feeling that I should leave something of my faith legacy for my grandchildren to read. My goal is to show Christian religious faith is following the example of Jesus Christ in a manner that becomes life transforming. I firmly believe there is a difference between following the example of Jesus and just believing the right things about Jesus.

There is also a third reason. This one may be the most important. I believe the fundamentalist mindset has done more to drive people from the church than anything else, especially young people. I cannot begin to count the number of people I have met over the years who told me they were raised in a Christian home, attended church, and now have nothing to do with it. When I asked why, their answer generally referred to their inability to equate what they were told they had to believe with how they actually believed things to be. When they described the God in which they didn't believe, I could generally agree with them. I didn't believe in that God either. I hope what I have written will give those individuals a different look at what it means to be a Christian. People continue to leave the church because their hearts cannot worship what their minds cannot believe.

There were many persons influential in my faith journey. First, I need to mention my parents, Glen and Helen Pember, who raised me in a Christian home. I can remember my mother reading the Bible to me and me asking her questions. It seems my questioning began at an early age. One particular discussion was about hell. She believed in it literally, and I was telling her how I could hide from the fire. This was an interesting discussion I still remember. Mom was the third daughter of Katie and Jacob Steinert. She was raised Lutheran and learned her catechism in the German language in a small church in Kansas. I

HOW IT ALL BEGAN

don't believe she ever left behind what she learned, although when she married my dad, she became a Baptist. She was always more tolerant of other denominations than my dad. I believe it had a lot to do with her experience of growing up in one denomination and spending her adulthood in another. She saw the good in both.

My dad was somewhat lacking when it came to tolerance of other denominations or anyone in his denomination with whom he disagreed. That may be too strong a statement. He tolerated them but knew they were all wrong. It is interesting to note he started his Sunday school training in a Methodist-Episcopal church, now a United Methodist congregation. It is where his parents attended in his early years. That ended when his parents were "converted" in a revival meeting at the local Baptist church. From that point on Dad's religion was Baptist. There were a number of years when he was not active at all, until a minister who somehow appealed to him brought him back into the fold. From that time on the Baptist faith could not be wrong, or at least his understanding of it could not be in error. The Baptist church about which I speak was part of the old Northern Baptist Convention, now known as American Baptist Churches, USA. I like to tell people it is the "liberal" Baptist convention. Sometimes the explanation they understand best is when I tell them it is "Yankee Baptist." That seems to be understood in contrast to "Southern Baptist." The truth is, the church in which I received my early religious training could probably have fit equally well in the Southern Baptist Convention, the Conservative Baptist Convention, or any equally conservative Baptist group.

My early religious training was definitely Baptist fundamentalism. I remember attending two weeks of revival meetings every autumn and always having difficulty staying awake. Most often there was some loud preaching, long sermons, and long, drawn-out invitations. I don't remember many conversions, but always a lot of rededications at the end of the two weeks. After all, when you don't have much in the way of conversions, you need something to show for two weeks of revival meetings.

I do remember one sermon that had a lasting impression on me.

The sermon was titled, "The Train to Hell." This train's cars held different groups of people. Some I remember were a car with dancers, a car with card players, a car with smokers, and a car for drinkers—all headed for hell. This was a significant sermon to me because of what happened. Dad took the visiting evangelist to a neighboring city to arrange for a revival meeting there. Dad noticed the evangelist kept rolling down the window so he could spit. You see, he was chewing tobacco. You guessed it. There was no car on the train for tobacco chewers. This is one of my earliest memories of an inconsistency in preaching and living. Of course, he did have the "correct beliefs." Who said it was supposed to transform his life? This sermon came to mind often when I wondered how people could claim to be Christian and act in ways that seemed to be inconsistent with what they claimed to believe. That was before I realized it was not "correct beliefs" but transformed behavior that was a better measure of a Christian.

One example will illustrate the theological climate of this Baptist church. Due to a shortage of teachers, our minister was asked to teach science classes in the high school. This was during World War II, when there was a shortage of teachers. He was talking to my dad about teaching science. Dad asked the minister what he taught about creation. He answered that he told them what the textbook said, and then told them how it really happened. To translate, he taught them the theory of evolution out of the book, and then told them the way it really happened: God created the world in six days. This is not to disparage the minister, as he had a very positive influence on me. It is rather to give a sense of the theological climate at this Baptist church. One thing was perfectly clear: the church of my childhood certainly had God and my beliefs neatly boxed for me.

There were numerous Sunday school teachers and pastors who left their imprint on me, and I can't begin to name them all. I probably should say that most of them would disown me now based on where my faith journey has led me. My attendance at some type of Christian summer camp from the ages of nine through nineteen also had a significant influence on me. Most of the counselors and ministers I met

HOW IT ALL BEGAN

in those experiences would probably disown me now. I have used "disown" twice in this paragraph, and it may be the wrong word to use. More likely, those I said would disown me would simply tell me I was wrong, feel sad, be deeply disappointed, and try to bring me back to the "correct beliefs." Some would tell me I was wrong and be concerned about where I would spend eternity.

As I look back, what I gained from all of them were not the "correct beliefs" they were attempting to impart. In their lives I sometimes saw the "correct beliefs" were the most important thing, because I couldn't see any transforming effect on their lives. The way some lived their lives while claiming to hold "correct beliefs" almost caused me not to become a minister. If what they did over against what they said was Christianity, I wanted nothing to do with it. The word "hypocrisy" is sometimes used to describe such behavior. In some of them I did see a dimension in their lives that was transforming. Their examples stayed with me.

College, seminary, and my first (and only) civilian pastorate all impacted me. In college I must give credit to a college biology professor who first introduced me to an excellent explanation of what evolution was all about. In a required college religion class, I heard for the first time that it was all right to be a Christian and believe in evolution. In another class on religion I encountered the possibility of doubt being the growing edge of faith. This was heresy! A Christian did not doubt—or so I had been told. What I experienced was that it was not just a possibility, for it was happening in me. That was an eye opener, and it fit! From this you can probably deduce I went to college without much influence other than fundamentalist Christianity. In my knowledge of religious beliefs, other than what I had been taught growing up, I was extremely naïve.

In seminary I owe much to my New Testament professor. So often I remember him giving different approaches to a particular issue and then ending by saying, "You pays your money and you takes your choice." My religious education professor talked about Christian nurture, saying that it was possible for a child to be raised in a Christian home never knowing the time he/she was not Christian. What a contrast from being raised with the concept that you had to have a "conversion experience" and be "saved" to be truly Christian.

One other item needs to be mentioned about my education. A pastor of my home church thought I was wasting my time going to college. All I needed was a call from God and my Bible. On one occasion when I was home from college, he preached a sermon on the apostle Peter. Peter didn't go to college, he didn't go to seminary, and he probably had very little formal education, but look at him. He answered Jesus' call for disciples and became the greatest of them all. It may not have been directed at me, but I felt as if it was. It succeeded in making me more determined than ever to complete college and go on to the seminary.

An important influence right after seminary was the pastor of a local church on the San Francisco Peninsula. I was a member of a group of clergy who met every Friday morning for breakfast, study, discussion, and personal reflection. One series of studies was given by this pastor. I can't even tell you what all the topics were, but I can tell you they presented an entirely different way of looking at Christianity than I had experienced, even in seminary. They struck a chord within me. I think it gave me my first permission that it was okay, and I wouldn't go to hell for shuffling beliefs in my God box. I have sometimes said in seminary I was like a sponge, trying to soak up everything poured on me. After seminary I started to squeeze the sponge to see what would come out. This pastor was one who helped me squeeze the sponge. I like to think I continue to squeeze the sponge regularly.

On my tour in Vietnam I met a missionary who belonged to a fundamentalist denomination. I have to admit he destroyed any stereotype I may have had of his denomination, and I did have some. We got into a theological discussion and I don't remember how it happened. I do know in similar situations I avoided theological discussions because we were generally miles apart. In the course of our discussion, he told me he believed the second coming of Christ was best explained as what happens when a person after conversion feels the Holy Spirit come into

HOW IT ALL BEGAN

his/her life. I knew at that point there was hope for the world. I decided he was a missionary because he did not have to deal with all the theological issues within his denomination. Those are my words, not his.

Reading has become more important to me over the years. I do have to admit I didn't do nearly enough in my earlier years. I believe I made up for it after I retired from the Army. There were many authors whose writings had an influence on me. Early influences were Peter A. Bertocci, *Introduction to the Philosophy of Religion;* Dr. Leslie Weatherhead, *The Christian Agnostic;* Dr. Harry Emerson Fosdick, *A Guide to Understanding the Bible;* John A. T. Robinson, *Honest to God;* Joseph Fletcher, *Situation Ethics;* and L. Harold DeWolf, *A Case for Theology in Liberal Perspective.* More recently I have read books by Bishop John Shelby Spong, Marcus Borg, Karen Armstrong, John Dominic Crossan, Elaine Pagels, John Polkinghorne, Bart D. Ehrman, Gregory J. Riley, and more of John A. T. Robinson. My reading has not been restricted to these authors and has included many others. The above authors have been the most influential and are probably the best known. I can identify with what they say. They have helped me squeeze the sponge and made it all right for me to have thoughts "outside the box."

Those familiar with the authors listed above might say I only read one approach to issues. To the contrary, I read many books with which I do not agree. They may not appear in the list because they had no positive influence on me. These included books by self-proclaimed atheists, books by Hal Lindsay, as well as W. A. Criswell's *Why I Preach That the Bible Is Literally True.* Quite frankly, I don't read an overwhelming number of these types of books. I seem to have difficulty leaving my brain somewhere else when I read them and what they are telling me I have to believe.

So where do I stand theologically? Throughout my career I worked with quite a number of alcoholics. An alcoholic who has stopped drinking is referred to as "a recovering alcoholic." Using that idea I will call myself "a recovering fundamentalist." I was there once, but am not there any longer. I definitely do not consider myself a fundamentalist.

One of my definitions of a fundamentalist is appropriate to state at this point. On one of my assignments as an Army chaplain, I went in to speak with the executive officer (XO) of my unit about an issue on which we disagreed. I was very confident that the new factual information I had could change his mind. Much to my disappointment, he discounted all I presented and maintained his position. I could not understand how he could so blatantly ignore what I had presented. When I came out of his office I lamented to the adjutant my disappointment. He said to me, "Chaplain, don't you know when the XO has made up his mind, you cannot confuse him with the facts?" That comment has never left me, and I have since applied it to anyone who I think is not listening to reason. More particularly, I apply it to the fundamentalist mindset. A fundamentalist is one who, having made up his or her mind about something regarding scripture or the Christian faith, cannot be confused with the facts. For example, a belief in the inerrancy of scripture cannot be confused with all the facts provided by critical biblical scholarship of the last two hundred years which says it just isn't that way. This is a mindset that promotes absolutism, the belief that, "The way I see it is the way it is…period!" The God of this mindset is often seen as wrathful, demanding, vengeful, and unforgiving, to name just a few traits. You don't want to be on his wrong side. This God can also be a loving God, but only if the rules are followed completely and absolutely—plus a combination of "correct beliefs." The fundamentalist reserves the right to decide what these rules are, generally preceded by the words, "God said…" They never catch on it is what they are saying God said, not necessarily words from the mouth of God. At the same time, what better way to foster strict obedience than to use God as your authority? One of my disagreements with them is that they do not grant anyone else this same right to decide. They have their God box, and no one is going to change what is in it!

In addition to being a recovering fundamentalist, I sometimes refer to myself as a Christian agnostic. I first heard that term as the title of one of the books I read. At that point, I wasn't even sure what it meant. Now I think I am one. The term is shocking to some people. They hear "agnostic" and immediately equate it with "atheist." That is far from the truth; atheist I am not. An agnostic is literally a "not knower." There are many things that reference scripture and the Christian faith that I do not know and am not bothered by it. I don't know what happens after death. I have my theories, but cannot prove them, so really I don't know. Anyone who tells you they absolutely know what will happen after death is not being truthful. I would be very willing to have anyone prove to me they know what happens beyond any doubt. I'm talking facts, not suppositions. Someone telling me I just have to accept it on faith doesn't answer the question. Such a statement tells me that person doesn't know either! I guess I am also a little like Mark Twain, who said words to the effect, "It's not the parts of the Bible I don't understand that bothers me, it's the parts I understand and do nothing about." Another term that is beginning to gain ground is "Progressive Christianity." I like that term and I could probably fit into that category. I like the term "Christian agnostic" better, as it gets attention immediately. Progressive Christianity doesn't readily resonate with many people.

If you proceed on beyond this point, prepare yourself to encounter thoughts definitely not residing inside the box of traditional Christianity. Some of the thoughts I present already exist. Most of you have heard the phrase "There is nothing new under the sun." A lot of truth is behind that statement. I do believe different people see the sunlight reflected in different ways. I may present some existing thoughts in a little different way. Do any of these thoughts have the slightest possibility of becoming part of accepted Christian thinking in the future? If not, then why not? Read on, then you decide.

2

THE BIBLE: WORD OF GOD OR GOD'S WORDS?

In the late nineteenth century, Darwinism was seen as a threat to conservative Christianity. In an attempt to counter this threat, Bible conferences were held across the United States to rally the true adherents of the faith. In 1895, in Niagara Falls, New York, a Conference of Conservative Protestants was convened. An outgrowth of this conference was the issuing of five principles necessary for anyone claiming to have the "correct beliefs." In the early 1900s, there were a group of pamphlets printed that were based on these principles and referred to as "The Five Fundamentals." It is generally accepted that it was at this point the word "fundamentalist" became a part of our vocabulary. Then, as also now, the word refers to a particular mindset and is not tied to any one denomination. The money to print these pamphlets was donated by Lyman Stewart, who founded what was then the Union Oil Company of California. They were first mailed to 300,000 Christians around the world and later were published in twelve volumes of essays. The adherents to these fundamentals of Christianity came to be called fundamentalists. The Five Fundamentals list is as follows:

1. The Bible is the literal, inerrant word of God.

THE BIBLE: WORD OF GOD OR GOD'S WORDS?

2. Jesus was literally born of a virgin.
3. Jesus died on the cross as a substitutionary atonement for our sins.
4. The miracles of Jesus recorded in the New Testament literally happened.
5. The resurrection of Jesus was a literally physical resuscitation, he literally ascended into heaven, and there will be an actual "second coming," when he will return to earth.

Earlier, I said if you did not consider yourself to be a fundamentalist, but believed certain things, you probably were a fundamentalist. The above list is certainly a good starter for you to evaluate your theological position. Remember, if it looks like a duck, walks like a duck, and quacks like a duck, it probably is a duck.

In discussions with fundamentalist believers, I am sometimes asked if I believe the Bible to be true. I tend to view that as a trick question and believe there is a question behind the question—whether I believe the Bible to be the inerrant, literal words of God. Most of the time my answer is to ask what they mean by "believe."

I believe faith is a growth process, and my growth has been from being as rabid a fundamentalist as you can be to where I am now. Before I talk more specifically about fundamentalism, I want you to know I have been there. I do not write based on what others have told me, but based on what I have believed, what I felt, what I now believe, and what I now perceive in discussing beliefs with fundamentalists.

Religious fundamentalism is basically oppressive. This is true of all fundamentalist religious faiths, and Christianity is not an exception. Religious fundamentalism is more often about controlling behavior than it is about teaching truth. Control is maintained by making sure followers know what will happen to them if they dare to deviate even one iota from stated fundamental beliefs. The issue of "correct beliefs" becomes more important than behavior. For Christians, being faithful means holding to a certain set of "correct beliefs" about the Bible, Jesus, and God. The most faithful Christians are those who hold rigidly to the inerrancy and infallibility of those "correct beliefs." Fundamentalists often use the words "fact" and "belief" interchangeably. If it is a "belief" it must be a "fact." In all reality, a "belief" may not be a "fact." Not all things contained in fundamentalists' "correct beliefs" about scripture are facts. That doesn't bother them too much: what can't be proven you just accept on faith. You accept it even if it can be factually proven to be in error. Beliefs begin to break down when you are more concerned with "Did it happen?" rather than with "What does it mean?"

I read in scripture, "*...and you will know the truth, and the truth will make you free.*" (John 8:32). I'm not sure I have ever met a "free" fundamentalist. I think the knowledge of truth and the freedom it can bring is scary to those who hold to a rigid, unquestioned, unwavering set of religious beliefs. It is certainly a threat to the gurus who want to keep followers within the "correct belief" system. This I would say is true of any religion or faith group. I believe these people live in fear that too much freedom would destroy the house of cards containing their beliefs. They live in fear of finding out the truth, not in freedom through knowledge of truth. I can speak to that personally. I have been there.

Because of challenges while I was in seminary, I was forced to ask myself a very difficult question. There I was, studying to become a minister. I reached a point where it became necessary for me to be honest and ask, "If I wasn't afraid of what would happen to me if I wasn't a Christian (eternally speaking), would I still be a Christian, much less planning to become a Christian minister?" The answer did not come overnight, and wrestling with the question brought me face-to-face with what I call the "fear factor." I was forced to admit I was a Christian because I was afraid of God and what God would do to me if I wasn't. I had been indoctrinated well in my fundamentalist religious education while growing up. I came to the realization that God was to be loved, not feared. The verse "God is love" took on new meaning for me. I was to live as a recipient of God's love, not God's wrath. That put a whole new spin on why I was a Christian and studying to

THE BIBLE: WORD OF GOD OR GOD'S WORDS?

become a minister. I never looked back. Being Christian became the way I chose to live because of personal choice, not because I was afraid of what would happen if I didn't. What a freeing experience and what new insights I have discovered over the years. To me it is an ongoing process. I'm not there yet—and never will be. I would wish that all fundamentalists could be recovering fundamentalists. Unfortunately, that is like wishing I would win the lottery.

The controlling concept of going to hell creates such a fear that many fundamentalist adherents will not even read an article or book if they see anything that indicates the author or content will not support the inerrancy and infallibility of the Bible. And what is it they fear? A big fear is that the Devil is tempting them and trying to lure them away from the true faith.

Belief in an eternal hell in the hereafter is a tremendous motivator for zealous fundamentalists whether they are laity or clergy. My first parish after seminary was starting a new church. I attended a three-day conference about what to do and how to do it when starting a new church. One of the presenters was a minister from Southern California who had one of the fastest growing new churches in his area. After his presentation, he was asked about his approach to people when he went out calling on newcomers in the neighborhood. He said, "When I stop in front of their house, I visualize the family burning in hell. That motivates me to call on them and explain to them how they can be saved."

Tripp York, in his book, *The Devil Wears Nada*, quotes Bill Hicks as follows: "Christianity has a built-in defense system: anything that questions a belief, no matter how logical the argument is, it is the work of Satan by the very fact that it makes you question a belief." I would narrow that statement to fundamentalist in particular rather than Christians in general. If believers question anything about "correct beliefs," then they are surely headed for eternal hell in the hereafter.

Fundamentalists like to demonize those who point to discrepancies and contradictions in scripture. They warn followers against reading anything that would even hint of discrepancies or contradictions. Followers are informed their faith will be destroyed and they will become victims of the wrath of God. Those scare tactics work on a lot of people and keep them under control. A good deal of guilt is also mixed into the equation. Followers are indoctrinated in such a way that to even think about straying outside the defined "correct beliefs" brings on feelings of guilt. The guilt is caused by daring to even question what you have been told is The Truth

Fundamentalists don't seem to believe that rational, critical thinking can be a part of the Christian faith. The clue is in the word "critical." If in doubt (a terrible thing for a fundamentalist to admit, which is different from saying they never have doubts), you don't search for answers. They would be very much in agreement with the words of a second century African convert, Tertullian. Elaine Pagels, in her book, *Revelations*, quotes him as saying, "Questions make people 'heretics' and demands that his hearers stop asking questions and simply accept the 'rule of faith.'" The question that always must be asked is who determines the correct "rule of faith," or as I like to call it, "correct beliefs." It is almost as if denial of knowledge makes faith strong, and increase of knowledge makes faith weak. Besides, a fundamentalist doesn't have to search for truth—they already have it all! There is nothing more arrogant than a fundamentalist who has the truth, the whole truth, and nothing but the truth. When I was in college I had a much older but very devout and fundamentalist Christian say to me, "The longer you go to school the dumber you get!" This was in response to a discussion we were having in which I was relating new insights I had gained concerning the Bible. These insights had been gained in college courses I was currently taking. If there seems to be a contradiction found in scripture, you don't seek or question. You accept what the fundamentalist gurus tell you to believe (and you better believe it—remember, hell is waiting for you).

Who are these gurus? Topping the list are old-time Christians, who always know more than any young whippersnapper Christians. Included are teachers and preachers of the fundamentalist persuasion. Keep in mind that the way to keep you in line (apart from the hell threat) is to treat you in the same way mushrooms are grown. You grow

THE BIBLE: WORD OF GOD OR GOD'S WORDS?

mushrooms by keeping them in the dark and feeding them lots of manure. The gurus don't want you to question any "correct belief." Soren Kierkegaard was a nineteenth century Danish philosopher/theologian. He is sometimes referred to as the father of existentialism as well as modern psychology. He said, "There are two ways to be fooled. One is to believe what isn't true; the other is to refuse to believe what is true."

I'm not willing to put my trust in any belief that cannot undergo the scrutiny of being questioned. A questioning of the inerrancy and infallibility of scripture through historical textual criticism will prove inerrancy, and infallibility can be easily disproven but can never be proven. Wherever there is denial, there is dysfunction, and fundamentalist faith becomes more closed and blind. Again I reiterate, you don't question, you just accept "correct beliefs" on faith. In my opinion this is the major reason why many young people raised in a fundamental faith throw over Christianity completely. They have learned how to think critically. Fundamentalism does not allow you to think critically about any aspect of "correct beliefs." Acquiesce, but not think.

I offer a word of caution. Beware of any preacher, guru, elder, charismatic person, Sunday school teacher, or Bible study leader who informs you they have the true interpretations of scripture. Saying it another way, they tell you they have the ultimate truth. Put a warning label on them. They are about to take you into their territory. It might be territory that will stymie your spiritual growth. If you accept it, you will have a set of "correct beliefs." You will have all the correct answers, even though they may not stand up to a critical review.

In Matthew's gospel, Jesus is asked which commandment is the greatest. He replied, *"You shall love the Lord your God with all your heart, and with all your soul, and with all your mind."* (Matthew 22:37). I have heard much about saving souls and having Jesus come into your heart in fundamentalist preaching. I can't recall ever hearing too much about using your mind! I also find it rather difficult to carry on a conversation with a fundamentalist concerning questions about the Christian faith. I am always seeking new ideas and new approaches to scriptures and the Christian faith. Fundamentalists are fearful of seekers unless what you seek is their interpretation of truth. They would never categorize it as their interpretation of truth. What they proclaim IS the truth—period! Elizabeth Burns, who went from being a party girl alcoholic to being a Christian, wrote in her book, *The Late Liz*, the following: "I find I only like the seekers, those who are forever seeking. The rest, the ones who've found and settled, and the ones who don't look at all, I do not like. I can see I'll have to learn to love them but I'll never like them."

All believers have doubts. The difference is between those who admit it and those who do not. You can generally identify those who won't admit it by their rigid pronouncements of the "correct beliefs" they espouse. Doubt to those who admit it can become a growing experience that strengthens faith. Doubt to those who are unable to admit it is a terrifying experience. Many are indoctrinated to believe if you have doubts it is probably Satan tempting you and trying to lure you away from the Christian faith. To admit doubt is tantamount to losing and destroying faith, rather than strengthening it.

Sara Brunsvold, in an article written for "Faith Walk" in the June 16, 2012 issue of the *Kansas City Star*, discussed what she considers to be the benefits of doubt. When younger, it was emphasized to her that if she doubted or questioned anything about her faith, she was really denying her faith. That concept didn't sit well with her, and she writes that she tried to hide her questioning. "…I pretended the questioning didn't happen, lest I myself begin to believe I'm not a believer…" She goes on to relate how she came to the realization that questioning her faith never caused her to lose it, but actually strengthened it. I couldn't have said it any better. She identifies what I believe happens to many people. Her comment "…I pretended the questioning didn't happen, lest I myself begin to believe I'm not a believer…" illustrates the point. Because fundamentalists are so indoctrinated to believe, questioning the faith means losing or leaving the faith, which is exactly what they do. They decide that if they have questions, it must be because they no longer believe, so they vote with their feet—out the door of their faith group.

It is my firm belief how you view the Bible has the biggest impact on where your belief system will take you. That makes scripture a good

THE BIBLE: WORD OF GOD OR GOD'S WORDS?

place to start on the issues. We have our God box, which contains our opinion of how to view the Bible. Conflict relating to one's view of the Bible is one of the biggest issues dividing Christians today. I like to think the division is probably along the lines of whether we see the Bible as of human origin or of divine origin. Is the Bible God's words, or God's word? There is a big distinction between the two. To view the Bible as God's words is literalism, a basic tenet of fundamentalist belief. To see the Bible as God's word is to see the message or truth conveyed by the written words. This approach may say different things to different generations.

Fundamentalism sees the Bible as of divine origin, inerrant and infallible. This is the belief that God dictated and man wrote. Therefore, whatever is contained in its pages are "the words of God." Fundamentalists believe the Bible says what it means, means what it says, and that does it! I sometimes see a bumper sticker that sums up that approach very well: "God said it; I believe it; that does it!" They would proclaim that experts are not needed to tell us what God wants us to hear. Furthermore, we must take it seriously because it comes directly from God. Those who adhere to this idea would probably say "Amen" to W. A. Criswell's book, *Why I Preach That the Bible Is Literally True*. To those dear souls, I simply say that I am sorry they left their brains in the vestibule when they entered the sanctuary. To say the Bible is literally true poses many questions that I will say more about later. Suffice it to say at this point there are different accounts of the same events and contradictions within the pages of the Bible. It takes some real mental gymnastics and contortions to reconcile them all as literal, to prove an inerrant Bible. There are laws followed by ancient people that just have no meaning in today's world. Of course, when you anesthetize your brain, it is possible to rationalize anything.

A primary concern in fundamentalist interpretation is finding ways to prove the events or words are literal historical events. Fundamentalists have no understanding of the concept that not taking the Bible literally does not mean you don't take it seriously. Fundamentalists do not accept that myth and metaphor are not lies, but illustrate meaning much more important than "Did it really happen; is it historical?" Truth need not be limited to fact. I read somewhere when an American Indian storyteller would begin to relate a story, the beginning would often be something like this: "I don't know if these events actually happened, but I know the story is true." A story need not be historical to contain truth. This is a concept entirely foreign to the fundamentalist mind when applied to the Bible.

The fundamentalists sincerely believe it is their duty to protect scripture from being tainted by false interpretation—any interpretation that disagrees with fundamentalist interpretation. This creates real difficulties when trying to discuss religion with fundamentalists who presume to have the truth, the whole truth, and nothing but the truth. This is the arrogance I mentioned earlier. What is interesting is that not even all fundamentalists can agree on what constitutes truth. Their thinking is dangerous because what they think becomes not merely their opinion, but God's words and God's opinion! Again, I emphasize they are unable to grasp the idea that if you don't take the Bible literally, it doesn't mean you don't take it seriously. For the fundamentalist, inerrancy of the Bible and a literal reading of any story in scripture is the starting point and then you can go from there. What if the story isn't literally true? Try to convince a fundamentalist it isn't. They fail to see the main point, being the truth behind the story, not the story itself. If you really want to raise a storm, refer to any historically unproven biblical story as a religious myth.

As a young adult with very fundamentalist beliefs, I saw myself as a defender of the faith. I was ready to take issue with anyone who disagreed with me. What I now realize is that my behavior seems to have been right in keeping with being a good fundamentalist. Fundamentalists love to have an enemy to fight in defense of the faith. No doubt in centuries past this played a major role as the Crusaders went forth to battle and destroy the enemies of the faith. This allows them to show their passion in fighting whatever they consider to be wrong. Very often this enemy is the Devil or Satan, or whatever other name you prefer. This enemy actually takes responsibility away from the one who has erred

THE BIBLE: WORD OF GOD OR GOD'S WORDS?

(sinned). It is Satan who blinds the eye of the one who disagrees with the fundamentalist literal interpretation of scripture. It is Satan who causes the unwary to sin, or sometimes the not so unwary. I like the quip I once heard, "Get thee behind me, Satan—and push!" I remember one story I heard about the evangelist Jimmy Swaggart's fall. He was caught with a prostitute. The story was that his ministry was doing so much good, Satan launched a counterattack. He lured him into a trap in order to strike a blow against his ministry. That is a sad explanation. Even sadder is that there were people who believed it.

The enemy doesn't stop there. It might be a rival church, whose minister "does not preach the word." In seminary, I purchased gas for my car from a gas station owned by a layperson who gave seminary students a discount. We frequently had discussions about theology and differences between his denomination and mine. On one occasion, our discussion centered on new church starts. He told me his denomination never started a new church in places where another church already existed. I told him I knew of at least two communities where there were plenty of churches and his denomination did come in and start a new church. I can remember his reply almost verbatim. "That's true," he said, "but only in those instances where the existing churches are not preaching the Word."

And we sure can't forget the religious liberals, the secular humanists, the communists, the new progressive Christians, members of other major faith groups other than Christian, and the media. Any perceived opposition becomes an incarnation of evil and takes on the face of the enemy. If you are good enough—or maybe I should say bad enough—you might even be declared an antichrist (1 John 2:18, 22). You do have to be a big threat to gain that distinction. Always keep in mind that the perception of a fundamentalist is the reality of a fundamentalist. Evil can actually become any person who has a thought or idea that does not agree with the fundamentalist interpretation of the "correct beliefs" one must hold. Fighting this enemy allows the believer to express righteous indignation (disguised anger). I fail to understand how so much anger (righteous indignation) can come from those who claim to be Christian. One result of this is that it allows people outside the church to discount the community of the faithful because they see no evidence "They will know we are Christians by our love."

Another part of the story for many fundamentalists is that the correct version of the Bible is extremely important. Generally the correct version has to be the King James Version, and not even the New King James Version. It helps if it happens to be a Scofield Version of the King James, as Scofield's notes become just part of the scriptures. A participant in a Bible study I was leading once told me that my Bible was leaving out some of the scripture. Upon further exploration, I found out what mine didn't have were Scofield's notes. The person who questioned me had a Scofield Bible and also considered Scofield's notes as scripture. It was this same person who shocked me with another comment. I had jokingly referred to a person who in a discussion about various translations had said, "If the King James Version was good enough for Paul, it is good enough for me!" The shocking retort was "That's what I believe!"

On a different occasion I was leading a group discussing various denominational beliefs. I mentioned that I considered myself to be a Christian (faith group, not denomination) first and my denominational preference second. One person in the group took issue with me and proclaimed quite proudly that she was a Baptist first and a Christian second. Such is the life of a fundamentalist!

The fundamentalists do not want to disturb the security they find in a literal interpretation of the Bible. One chip out of the wall and the whole house will fall down. They fear if they concede to even one error or contradiction in scripture, it will lead to the destruction of their entire faith. How can you be secure if you don't believe it all? God will certainly wreak his vengeance on you if you stray one iota from the "correct beliefs." That is certainly what happens when faith is based more on having "correct beliefs" than on being transformed by following and practicing the example set by Jesus Christ. Again, I emphasize the fundamentalist cannot see how you can believe in the truths of the Bible if you don't believe in its inerrancy and inspiration.

THE BIBLE: WORD OF GOD OR GOD'S WORDS?

From what I have said, you might think I believe fundamentalists are bad people. That is not what I think. I do think they are fearful people who are very sincere in what they believe and what they fear. I also believe there are some excellent con artists among fundamentalists. The con is in convincing you that hell is in your future if you don't buy their product. They may even stretch things somewhat to get you to buy the con. The con shows up in how they interpret scripture to support their con. In their mind, that also is all right. After all, anything you can do to save another from the fires of hell is legitimate. Saving sinners is a calling in which the end seems to justify the means. What is missing in their repertoire is the true meaning of grace. They believe God is out to get you if you aren't a true believer with "correct beliefs." Jesus came to proclaim to people that God loved everyone. Jesus came to proclaim a faith of forgiveness, not a faith of fear of hell and damnation. I believe true faith should never be about fear, but about grace and forgiveness—without any strings attached, including the string of walking down the aisle and being "saved."

An entirely different way of seeing the Bible is seeing it as written by humans but containing what can be considered the "word of God." Maybe a better word to use would be the "message" of God. It has its origin in the concept that the Bible is a human product in which the writers attempted to put in writing their understanding and experiences of God. This would make what they were saying not literally God's words, but metaphorically God's message. Is the message we can receive through reading their writings of value? This approach doesn't believe the scripture needs to be guarded; rather its message needs to be understood. The focus is not on "Did it happen?" but "What does it mean?" I don't believe the authors of the Old and New Testaments believed they were writing "God's words." Nor do I believe they perceived they were writing to future generations. They were writing to their contemporaries in their own time about their own issues. Putting it bluntly, a critical study of scripture reveals in many of its details that the Bible is absolutely downright wrong and contradicts itself!

Why are there such divergent views? To oversimplify it, some professional clergy have not done their best keeping congregations abreast of advancements and new discoveries in the field of biblical scholarship. And why is that? For some it is because they don't believe the advancements made in biblical research over the past 200 years. They may be self-taught, or they went to seminaries that didn't give credibility to biblical historical criticism and new discoveries. For others, it is a matter of security. If you want to continue as the minister of the church you are serving, you have to be careful what you bring to the attention of the congregation. People will go to a doctor and want the latest technology applied to whatever ails them. They not only want it; they demand it. The same people go to church and want to hear the tried and true (maybe not true but at least familiar) things they have heard from their youth on into adulthood. Trying to get them to think along new ideas can lead to them voting with their feet and/or their pocketbook. Either they leave, or the minister leaves!

An illustration might fit well at this point. Who was an early president of the United States who died as a result of medical technology of his time? It was our first president, George Washington. What was the medical technology that killed him? It was bloodletting, something that was guaranteed to get rid of whatever was bad in your body. President George Washington most likely bled to death as a result of his up-to-date medical treatment.

Now, my question is, who of you would go to a doctor that practices bloodletting as an important protocol in treating disease? I don't believe any of you would volunteer. Why not? Oh, you tell me that many discoveries and advancements have been made in the field of medicine. Why would you continue to hold religious concepts that date back to the time period of bloodletting and before? Why wouldn't you want to know and hear the latest in historical critical biblical research? Enough said.

It is generally accepted among scholars that there was no written scripture prior to the tenth century Before the Common Era (BCE). Many different authors put together the words of the Old Testament from about the middle of the tenth to the middle of the second century

THE BIBLE: WORD OF GOD OR GOD'S WORDS?

BCE. Most present-day scholars date the New Testament writings between 50 Common Era (CE) until early or mid-100 CE. What was there before that time? Oral tradition was what passed along the stories. If we do the math, that means the story of Abraham existed by word of mouth for 800 to 900 years before someone decided they needed something in writing. The fact that very few people could even read may have had something to do with oral tradition. I'm not sure how much inerrancy you can have in a 900-year-old story. I find it impossible to pass one simple sentence down a line of ten people and have it come out the same at the end as it started. And yes, I have read about oral tradition and how it works. I have also read how along the way there are those who decide to improve it or correct it by changing it just a wee bit. Multiple the "wee bits" by 900 years and it probably adds up to quite a bit.

Most people think of the Bible as a book, and a book it is, but it is more. In actuality, it is a collection of books, sixty-six books included in the Canon. Don't think sixty-six books means sixty-six authors. In reality, we don't know the number of authors who contributed to the sixty-six books. Some books had more than one author, and some authors wrote more than one book. Maybe they thought themselves inspired by God to write and maybe they didn't. In 1 Corinthians, Paul even makes a claim that some words he was saying were from himself, not from God. He was giving advice to the married and said, *"To the married I give this command—not I but the Lord…"* (1 Corinthians 7:10). Then a little later he says, *"To the rest I say—I and not the Lord—…"* (1 Corinthians 7:12). Does this mean that God inspired Paul to say he was not inspired? I add here that 1 Corinthians is not one of the books in dispute about whether Paul wrote it. Most biblical scholars accept most of it as his. I will mention some verses in question later. Again, I say it is doubtful if any scripture writers thought of themselves as writing God's literal words. I may be overreaching, but I am going to make a generality and say they basically all had a similar theme. They wrote about relationships between God and any who would follow him. They wrote about consequences of following or not following

GOD IN A BOX

God. They wrote about what they believed God expected of those who would follow him.

To explore further the issue of multiple authorships, we will look at the first five books of the Bible, known as the Pentateuch, Torah, or books of Moses. For years, authorship was attributed to Moses, notwithstanding the account given of his death. How do you write about your death after you are dead? The literalist would say God told Moses what was going to happen and Moses wrote it down. Could I sell you a good bridge? It is located in Brooklyn. Since at least the nineteenth century, scholars have known that the first five books were not the works of a single author. The most common belief is they were the works of at least four strands of Jewish authorship and were composed over a period of 500 years. It's not the scope of this writing to go into details about those four strands.

There is another element to keep in mind about biblical stories and science. In Bible times, Old and New Testaments alike, the universe was considered to be three-tiered, the heavens above, the flat earth, and the region below the earth. Over the centuries, scientific knowledge expanded and concluded there was a universe with other planets in it, the sun and moon being two prime examples. The prevalent belief placed the Earth at the center of that universe. Galileo and Copernicus both got into serious trouble with the church because they dared to question that view. God (or any god for that matter) was thought to dwell in or above the heavens.

Let us explore some ways of looking at scripture. We will start with the Old Testament. Keep in mind the Bible should not be considered either an accurate history book or a scientific textbook. Remember, those who wrote the Bible were not doing it because they believed they were writing down the "words of God" or history. They were writing down how they experienced God, and they were writing much more in a metaphorical sense than literal historical accuracy. Historical events may be alluded to, but not in the sense of writing literal history. They would probably be confused if they saw how many people in our present age want to make the words historical and literal, or sometimes

THE BIBLE: WORD OF GOD OR GOD'S WORDS?

prophetic for our age. Additionally, there are contradictions about the same event recorded in different places. In places where differences occur, which account contains the true "words of God"?

An easy example is recorded in the first two chapters of Genesis, which give two different accounts of creation. Genesis 1:1 – 2:4a gives an account of creation with a chronological order of everything being created before humankind, and then last of all, man and woman are created. Starting with Genesis 2:4b – 25, we see a different chronological order of creation. This is the account that introduces us to the Garden of Eden. In this account, man is created before other living creatures; then livestock, creatures, and birds were brought to man. He named them, but none were a suitable helpmeet, so God put man to sleep, took a rib from him, and made a woman. These are men's accounts of how they saw creation written in a metaphorical or symbolic sense, not God's account of how it really happened. Most ancient cultures had creation stories, so the writers of Genesis were up to date with their times. In no way are any of these accounts to be considered as some type of history or scientific evidence about how God created the world. For the fundamental literalist, how can both chronological orders be true?

Almost everyone has heard of the Ten Commandments. In our age, there are a lot of controversies on where they can be displayed. Did you know there are three versions given in the Old Testament? The oldest version is Exodus 34:1-29. Then we have Exodus 20:1-17. We move out of Exodus to Deuteronomy 5:1-21, which some scholars think was written the same time as the creation story mentioned above. Which of these is the correct account? Which of these contains the true "words of God"? Did you know those commandments referring to how to treat others were not written on how all people were to be treated? They were written to give guidance on how Israelites were to treat each other. The rules didn't apply to treatment of other people outside of the Jewish community. The way they slaughtered their enemies should be adequate proof of this for any doubters.

In Genesis there is the story of a great flood. Noah, his family, and the animals survived on the ark. Did you know that all ancient civilizations record a flood in their histories? The book of Genesis describes the flooding of the Earth. Genesis 7:11 tells us that water came from underground as well as from the heavens. This is hardly scientific fact. The whole Earth was covered by fifteen cubits of water, including the mountains. To be literally true, water would have had to be more than five miles deep covering the Earth. It is an amount of water that could never be absorbed by the Earth or evaporated by the sun. Is this story literal history and scientifically accurate? I offer another tidbit of information here. Did Noah take seven of every kind of clean animal and two of every unclean animal (Genesis 7:2), or pairs of both clean and unclean animals (Genesis 7:8-10)?

What would happen if the sun stood still? Is this even a logical question? If you literalize everything written down in the Bible, you would believe it could happen and did happen because the Bible says so. In the book of Joshua (Joshua 10:12-13) we are told the sun stood still in the sky so the Israelites could continue the slaughter of the Amorites without the interference of darkness. Never mind that what we now know about the universe makes this impossible. We now know the sun does not travel through the sky; the Earth revolves around the sun. If the Earth stopped rotating, gravitational effects would destroy it. This is another story based on pre-scientific conclusions.

I want you to consider another incident recorded in the Old Testament. Do you really believe God told Joshua to kill off all the inhabitants in the city of Jericho (Joshua 6:1-21)? What kind of a god would do something as horrible as that? It is certainly not one that fits my definition of a "God of love." Again, we have here a story derived from the author's understanding of how God was taking care of his people. Did he think he was writing history? Probably not. Rather, he was writing metaphorically about some event that took place, and the people believed God was in the event. A metaphorical story points beyond the content of an event. It points to a message that is greater than the elements of the event.

Sheol was considered a shadowy place, the place where the dead

THE BIBLE: WORD OF GOD OR GOD'S WORDS?

reside. It is that tier of the three-tiered universe located just below the surface of the Earth. We know it by reading Genesis 37:35, Numbers 16:31-33, and Amos 9:2 in the Old Testament. Mark 9:48, in the New Testament, refers to hell "...*where their worm never dies, and the fire is never quenched.*" How did we get there from Sheol? Some equate Sheol in the Old Testament to Hades in the New Testament, and Hades is equated to hell. One person took all this literally and went one step further. He determined the living area under the Earth where worms don't die and gave those dimensions as the actual space for Sheol—Hades—or hell. Sorry, I don't have the dimensions. Do be careful if you go digging for worms. You can never be sure what eternally damned spirit of a deceased person your shovel may hit!

There are other problems with a literal interpretation of Old Testament scripture. The fundamentalist is very selective about which verses to take literally. I believe sometimes it is simply because they don't realize the extent of the laws in the Old Testament and what it would mean if they tried to follow them literally. They readily point out homosexuality as a sin, and use Leviticus 18:22 and 20:13 as proof. Leviticus 20:13 says, *"If a man lies with a male as with a woman, both of them have committed an abomination; they shall be put to death; their blood is upon them."* What do you do with that one? The fundamentalists might very well agree with Leviticus. That is an easy one for them. What about Leviticus 24:16, which basically says anyone who blasphemes the name of the Lord must be put to death? They may even be okay with that if they have never cursed (show me the person). Any fundamentalist with a son may find the next one a little more difficult to take literally. What if the son is rebellious? Deuteronomy 21:18-21 gives the solution. The bottom line is to stone him to death. I wonder how long the literal application of scripture would appeal at this juncture.

There is one that any fundamentalist who has indoor plumbing—more precisely stated an indoor toilet—certainly must ignore. Deuteronomy 23:12-13 says: *"You shall have a designated area outside the camp to which you shall go. With your utensils you shall have a trowel;*

when you relieve yourself outside, you shall dig a hole with it and then cover up your excrement." Ask them how they handle that one! I can hear them say they didn't have indoor plumbing in that age. Of course they didn't. But the question becomes, "Are you a literal literalist or a literalist of convenience?"

There are many more examples. If you want more, read the books of Leviticus and Deuteronomy and see how much trouble you can get into with a literal view of scripture. You may also want to consider how many of them you are willing to take literally.

Sometimes I am asked, "Why is fundamentalism so prevalent in many of the new non-denominational churches, and why do they seem to have such phenomenal growth?" Behind that question seems to be the thought that if their approach wasn't correct, they wouldn't have such growth. A fast rate of growth does not always equate with fundamentalist theology. Neither does zeal necessarily equate with being correct. There are three reasons why I believe such churches—or any fast-growing church—experience growth considered above average. First, in all instances of which I am aware, they are or were led by very talented and charismatic leaders. Charismatic leaders attract followers. Second, they make newcomers feel very welcome and wanted. We all like to feel welcomed, especially in a church environment. Third, they give the impression they have all the answers. I can put that into three words: leadership, community, security.

All of us like answers to perplexing issues. We live in a very stressful time. It seems as if daily there are new crises that impact people's lives. People are filled with many anxieties in their daily lives and want answers for dealing with these stresses. Give them answers and they will come. This probably has been true of every age. In fundamentalist churches, those answers often are built around a literal interpretation of the Bible, a belief in the inerrancy of scripture and the infallibility of the word of God. What isn't talked about is the disillusionment that comes with the realization that the answers so hoped for aren't really answers at all. The answers are platitudes that are part of a fundamentalist belief system. Now here comes another kicker, which I

THE BIBLE: WORD OF GOD OR GOD'S WORDS?

mentioned earlier. To question anything shows a lack of faith, and you never want to show a lack of faith. What happens when you can't get answers to troubling questions and are discouraged from even asking them? Real disappointment can be the predicted outcome. The disappointment leads to an exit of members out the back door almost as quickly as newcomers are entering the front door.

I have already alluded to the fact that fundamentalists believe they do not interpret scripture, but just tell it like it is. Telling it like it is always has a slant to it, regardless of who is doing the telling. Whoever is reading the scripture text is not reading it in a vacuum. Sometime, somewhere, they have heard something about a particular scripture or the author of a particular book in the Bible, and it impacts what they read. If they never heard about or read scripture before, that too will have an impact. Much of what we get in interpretation takes place in some type of group setting. The setting could be family, a Sunday school class, a worship service, a friendly discussion, or any group that is studying scripture in some way. Whenever, however, and by whomever scripture is viewed, whatever insight is gained becomes an interpretation. The best interpretation comes when culture, place in history, author, and audience to whom it was written are also taken into account.

Many devout Christians would recoil at the thought that any scripture should ever be "interpreted." Their view is that it is very clear and plain in meaning, and interpreting adds to or subtracts from what is already there. Never mind that the words come from an entirely different age and culture. A story, probably not literal but nonetheless true metaphorically, relates the incident of a preacher who was reading the words in Matthew 8:12: "*...where there will be weeping and gnashing of teeth.*" A toothless parishioner asked this hellfire preaching pastor what would happen to those who had no teeth to gnash. "*Teeth will be provided*" was the preacher's answer. Of course, that was not interpretation; that was an explanation. The bottom line is, there will always be interpretation. The question is what kind of interpretation. It is interpretation that directs our understanding of the scripture. It should

GOD IN A BOX

be interpretation with an emphasis on what it means, rather than if it really happened.

Just for fun, let's look at some New Testament scripture, and let it just "tell it like it is," and see what it tells us. Let us be brave and start with the most important day in the calendar of the Christian year, Easter. Now we ask a simple question. "How many people were at the empty tomb?" Mark says a *young man* was present when *three women* arrived (Mark 16:1-5). If God dictated and man wrote, we should be able to stop here because it should be the same in every other Gospel. Guess what? Not correct. Matthew says it was *an angel* when *two women* arrived (Matthew 28:1-3). Maybe God forgot what he told the author of Mark. But there is more. Luke says those arriving at the tomb saw *two men*, and *doesn't number the women*, which could have been more than three (Luke 24:1-5). We still need to look at John's gospel as well. Maybe he can clear up the confusion. After all, his gospel was the last written, so he probably had read the other three and heard much more from oral tradition. John says *one woman* went to the tomb and rushed back to get *two disciples*, who went back to their homes. Mary stood crying outside the tomb and saw *two angels*; then she turned around and there stood *Jesus* (John 20:1-18). So if God dictated and man wrote, someone is confused! I have heard the argument from fundamentalists that the number of people present wasn't important. What was important was the happening. If you go there, it is no longer a literal reading and you are heading in my direction.

We need to add a few more items concerning the empty tomb. In both Matthew and Mark the women were told to go and tell (Mark 16:7, Matthew 28:7). Did they do that? Matthew says they did (Matthew 28:8), but Mark said they did not (Mark 16:8). You can't have it both ways. However you read it, one contradicts the other. And finally, what was the reaction of the disciples when they were told? There is no response listed in Matthew because Jesus met the eleven disciples on the mountain where he had told them to go (Matthew 28:16-17). Maybe Luke had the reaction correct. Who could believe a woman? Women had little standing, so it was considered nonsense

THE BIBLE: WORD OF GOD OR GOD'S WORDS?

(Luke 24:11). There certainly couldn't have been a response in Mark, because the women didn't tell anyone. Perhaps John had it right, saying that when they heard about it, Peter and another disciple ran to the tomb to see for themselves (John 20:3-4).

We could continue to list contradictions and discrepancies. For those who want to read the scriptures as inerrant and literal, they wouldn't read them anyway for fear of losing their faith. For those who are concerned more with "what does it mean" than "did it happen that way" we have already given enough information to make the point.

Women seem to have played a major role on that resurrection morning, so the subject of women would be an interesting place to go next. What is the attitude toward women in the Bible? Basically, women had no rights. They were the property of their father or husband. When a census was taken, only the men were counted. A revealing book to read in regard to the treatment of women is *The Harlot by the Side of the Road* by Jonathan Kirsch. It deals with Old Testament stories. I can hear the piety in the voice that tells me things are different in the New Testament. But are they really?

We go to 1 Corinthians 14:33-35: *"As in all the churches of the saints, women should be silent in the churches. For they are not permitted to speak, but should be subordinate, as the law also says. If there is anything they desire to know, let them ask their husbands at home. For it is shameful for a woman to speak in church."* These are the verses that most scholars don't believe are Paul's, but were added by someone later. But let's look at it as a literalist fundamentalist would. It's all God's words, so you ladies need to keep quiet. There would go a lot of Sunday school teachers, no public prayers from women, the choir would be a men's chorus, and there definitely would be no female clergy. You won't replace them easily. Except for a few denominations, I don't know many fundamentalist groups that hold to this as the letter of the law. Not doing so does cast into doubt the honesty of their literalism. Adding insult to injury is my statement that most scholars believe these words were not written by Paul. It is quite probable that women's keeping silent in the church is not the position held by Paul. It does contradict what he said earlier in 1 Corinthians 11:5: *"...any woman who prays or prophesies with her head unveiled disgraces her head—it is the same thing as having her head shaved."* Now I ask the fundamentalists, how it is possible for a woman to pray or prophesy if she is commanded to remain silent in the church?

Now let us look at I Timothy 2:8-15, the statement concerning women. Verses 8-10 speak about women's dress. Read literally, it says no jewelry, no permanents, and no fancy clothes. Read it in the context and culture in which it was written. It is saying, "Don't dress like the prostitutes." That is interpreting scripture by trying to determine what it means, not by whether it is literally true. Some other verses in 1 Timothy that seem to give a similar message to 1 Corinthians read, *"Let a woman learn in silence with full submission. I permit no woman to teach or to have authority over a man; she is to keep silent."* (1 Timothy 2:11-12). All I will say here is that it is almost unanimous agreement 1 Timothy is another of the books first attributed to Paul but now believed to have not been written by him. I say almost unanimous, because the inerrancy of the Bible group most likely would vehemently disagree.

One of the most controversial topics in our generation is the issue of homosexuality. One of the scriptures used against homosexuality is the story of Sodom and Gomorrah, Genesis 19:1-8. Seen in the context of that age, this is a story of gang rape. For whatever reason in that ancient culture, the humiliation of a man was best achieved by making him act like a woman in the sex act. This was done to insult his dignity. Thus humiliation, rather than male homosexual lust, is behind this story.

The real tragedy is what is often overlooked in this story. How did Lot try to keep his visitors safe from the crowd? He offered the crowd his virgin daughters in their place. This puts a little more icing on the cake of our discussion about the place of women in the Old Testament. God must have thought that was all right, because Lot was considered righteous and was allowed to escape the destruction.

So how is the story used? To build a case against homosexuality, but

THE BIBLE: WORD OF GOD OR GOD'S WORDS?

nothing is said about the treatment of women. Hear me again when I say the issue was of humiliation, not of homosexual desire. If we read the whole story and take it literally, does it mean it is all right to offer your virgin daughter to a villain to protect a guest? How many of you would do that?

Let's look at one more item illustrating how ancient world views impact scripture. In both the Gospel of Luke and the Acts of the Apostles, the author refers to the ascension of Jesus, a story based on a three-tiered view of the universe. Quoting from Acts, *"…as they were watching, he was lifted up, and a cloud took him out of their sight."* (Acts 1:9). To the fundamentalist, Jesus rose through the canopy over the earth—the sky—through some opening to sit on the right hand of God in heaven. Taken literally, where would heaven be located? Maybe it's somewhere beyond the universe? Being literal again, if Jesus went up at the speed of light (I learned in physics it is a little over 186,200 miles per second or 700 million miles an hour), he probably still would not have reached the edge of our own galaxy. It has been estimated that there are more stars in our galaxy than human beings who have ever lived on Earth. Add to that, it is estimated there are more galaxies in our universe than there are stars in our single galaxy. So is the ascension to be taken literally? Please tell me where heaven and Jesus are. And another thing, when the Earth rotates, which way is up and in which direction is Jesus traveling?

While we are on the ascension, we may as well look at another example of a contradiction. What I find particularly interesting about this one is that it is a contradiction written by the same author, Luke. Keep in mind Luke is considered to have written both the Gospel of Luke and the Acts of the Apostles. Above I quoted a verse from the book of Acts concerning the ascension. What I didn't mention was earlier in the verse (verse 3) it indicates Jesus appeared to them during a period of forty days. So where is the contradiction? In his gospel, Luke writes the events all took place on the first day of the week: Easter. At the end of the day he was with the disciples. Luke writes, *"While he was blessing them, he withdrew from them and was carried up into heaven."*

(Luke 24:51). The question concerns the time line. Did Jesus ascend at the end of Easter Day or forty days later? That is a contradiction that must be dealt with if you are a believer in the inerrancy of scripture. I guess there is always the option of playing ostrich!

I recently ran across a quote from Tony Campolo. He is the author of several books and was professor of sociology at Eastern College in St. Davids, Pennsylvania. He is considered by many to be a leader in evangelical social action. The quote comes from words he spoke at a Southern Baptist Convention sometime in the 1980s. He said, "I spoke at the Southern Baptist Convention a couple of years ago and I opened up by saying, 'I don't know why you're worrying so much about the inerrancy of scripture; after you prove that it's inerrant, you're not going to do what it says anyway.'" Does that mean there is more interest in proving it is true than in doing what it says? Think about it. You decide.

I could go on with many more examples of errors and contradictions in the Bible, but of what use? If you are a fundamentalist, ten thousand illustrations would not change your mind, but if you are not, what I have given should suffice. If you are neither and are actually intrigued by the issues, there are a lot of books available dealing rather extensively with the subject, such as those by Bart Ehrman. Marcus Borg is another good source. Books by both men are listed in the bibliography.

I emphasize the importance of proceeding with caution. Do not use my words as proof the Bible has nothing of value to say. The Bible has a lot to say to every age and to every person who will read it. What I am saying is you should not get hung up on the historical and literal accuracy and miss the great truths. Remember, don't ask, "Did it really happen this way?" Ask instead, "What does it mean?" You may want to add, "What does it mean in my life today?" Word of God or God's words? You decide.

I want to tell you about Caleb. The actual events of this story never happened. Nevertheless, the story is true. Caleb was born into a

THE BIBLE: WORD OF GOD OR GOD'S WORDS?

suburban Midwestern community. From the time of his birth, he was taken to the local First Church, where his family was active. The members of this church knew they were not the only church in the world, but viewed other churches as not having the truth and missing the mark. The members of this church pretty much kept to themselves and were not involved in any activities that smacked of ecumenism. If you were to visit members of this church, you would not notice anything different about these people. They went about their daily activities, worked hard, were friendly to strangers, and considered themselves to be law-abiding citizens. And, as already mentioned, they considered themselves to have an edge on truth that was lacking in other churches. To keep this truth intact for their children, they even had their own school for grades kindergarten through twelve.

You would notice nothing different, unless you sat in on a math class in their school or encountered a math issue in a day-to-day activity with one of them. Then you would notice a very strange thing. To the people in this church, two plus two equaled three. Children were taught that two plus two equals three. Children at home were taught that two plus two equals three. In dealings with one another, two plus two equaled three. If an outsider had any involvement with a member of this church that involved numbers, it soon became apparent that such dealings were based on two plus two equaled three. If you wanted to deal with them, you had to accept that as fact. No other end result was acceptable.

Not only was two plus two equals three the law of their church, but the concept was rigidly enforced. It was never to be questioned. To question it was to commit a grievous sin against the God in whom they believed and served, as well as against their community. To question it was to place oneself in danger of some awful thing happening—the same thing that would happen if you questioned any other tenets of their faith. You were in danger of losing your faith completely. You placed yourself in danger of being consigned to the eternal fires of hell. To most of us, it would appear rather simple to prove two plus two equals four by simply putting up two objects, then two more objects beside them and counting—one…two…three…four. That would be logically sound, but also against the teaching of this church. Whenever a member of this church saw two objects with two other objects close by, the worst thing they could do would be to count them and see if they added up to three or four. Sometime in the past, the elders had decided two plus two equals three, and that was the law of the believers! It was never to be questioned! If you saw anything that might lead you to question it, you immediately looked away, closed the book, or did whatever you had to do to ignore what might possibly refute the law that two plus two equals three.

This was the religious community into which Caleb was born and indoctrinated. As Caleb grew older he became aware of the inconsistency of two plus two equals three. Every time he saw two objects beside two objects, he counted them and they always added up to four. This perplexed him and when he questioned anyone in his church or school, he was severely chastised and told to never go there! He was told if he went there, the whole world of his faith would crumble and he would suffer dire consequences. Caleb brought the subject up to his parents. They were shocked to hear he would even want to question the concept, and warned him to never let other members of their religious community know he had such thoughts. He was told he would be ostracized by all, and again they emphasized dire consequences. When his parents found out he had posed the question to his teachers, they lived in fear of being questioned by the elders about how they could have raised such a child who would question matters of faith. Surely his parents must have done something wrong for him to question what was accepted as common knowledge to all other members of the church. The answer he most often received to his question was that some things could not be explained; they just had to be accepted on faith. Two plus two equals three was one of those things.

Caleb had doubts, but realized it was better to keep them to himself. As time passed, Caleb grew in wisdom and stature, and upon completion of high school in his religious community's school, he went away to college. He was questioned about his choice of the college he

THE BIBLE: WORD OF GOD OR GOD'S WORDS?

chose to attend. Those from his church who attended college generally chose a college supported by churches across the land that held the same view as the church in which Caleb was raised—that view being two plus two equals three. Caleb had an inquisitive mind and wanted to expand his knowledge base. Much to the consternation of his parents and others in the church, he chose to attend a college that taught two plus two equals four.

Caleb was delighted and amazed he was not struck by lightning and nothing drastic happened to him when he approached things with a two-plus-two-equals-four perspective. Whenever he counted two plus two, he always came out with four. This caused him to wonder how many other things he had been told were also suspect. He also discovered that everything was more rational and believable if approached with this perspective. He came to the realization that faith was not about pretending questions do not exist. A strong faith was being willing to pose the questions and search for answers. He discovered that searching often revealed new truth that did not require "faith" to accept. He discovered that logic and rational thinking were not the enemies of faith, and it was not necessary to embrace nonsense as truth simply because it was needed to prop up allegiance to a certain held belief, be it religious or otherwise. He came to the conclusion there was a major error in the belief system of the church in which he had been raised. The major error was an inordinate claim to possess absolute truth.

Through his studies at the university, Caleb continued to learn new things. He felt quite confident about the new knowledge he had acquired. This did create a major problem for him. Whenever he returned home, his family and members of the church would harangue him with a barrage of questions. What proved most difficult to Caleb was not the questions, but the unwillingness to listen to his answers. Unless he was willing to answer two plus two equals three, the conversation came to a quick halt. In one sense, what Caleb had been told turned out to be true. If you questioned two plus two equals three, you were in danger of losing your faith. Those in his home church now knew Caleb had lost his faith. Caleb also knew he had lost faith in what he was told he had to believe. He had found something stronger and with more substance. Faith took on a new meaning for him. He knew questions did not end the world but opened up the world.

By the time he had earned his college degree, he knew he did not fit in the church or even his home. He found a job as far away from the place of his youth as he could. From that point on, he refused to have anything to do with any church. He had decided all churches believed two plus two equals three, or some variation. He knew two plus two did not equal three, so why should he waste his time trying to convince them of anything different? If asked about his religious affiliation, he answered "none." Deep down inside he believed there was something greater than himself, and certainly different from what he had been taught while growing up. He just didn't have the energy or inclination to pursue in the religious arena what it might be. He was also fearful that if he searched, he would find the same attitude he had experienced when growing up. "Come with us, we have all the answers!" He certainly wasn't ready for more of that. For Caleb, the decision was that he would no longer call himself religious. Because of his beliefs and feelings, he decided he would call himself spiritual. He decided he could be a very spiritual person without the trappings he perceived would come with committing himself to a particular religion. Caleb still viewed the church and religion as being more interested in control than in seeking truth and serving others. From that point on, he simply classified himself as one who was spiritual, but not religious.

3

I BELIEVE IN GOD: WHAT DOES IT MEAN?

Most people put God in a box. Along with God, they have a lot of other beliefs in the box, some of which I have already discussed. Even though it is impossible to put God in a box, people try to do it anyway.

We are all familiar with boxes. There are all types and shapes, and they have many uses. When we use boxes, they have to be able to hold whatever it is we are placing inside. Your "God box" holds whatever god you decide to place inside. Maybe it would be better to say that your God box holds your God beliefs, whatever they might be. That would be true regardless of your religious belief.

It would also be true if you consider yourself an atheist. If you are an atheist, you have to put something in the box in order to have something in which you don't believe. The sad thing is, most people build that box when they are very young, probably as a child in Sunday school. It may even be a box they inherited! The disaster is the God box for most people doesn't change much even into adulthood. We have the god in which we believe—or disbelieve—in a box constructed with the help of others, and no one else better mess with it. It may even have been stored for a while. There is a type of security in having that old God box around, even if it might be rough around the edges, and even

GOD IN A BOX

if you are no longer sure of the contents. You have an idea of what is in it, and you keep the lid on tight. The problem with that approach is the limitation on how one understands God. It also can drastically hinder any growth in the spiritual realm. The words of an old familiar tune comes to mind: "Give me that old-time religion, give me that old-time religion…it was good for my father, it was good for my mother, and it's good enough for me." But where is your input, and what is good enough for you? Do you have your own God box, or do you have one that was passed down from a previous generation? It might be a good idea to look and see what your God box contains.

We can get very defensive about our God box. We may not even be sure of all that is in it, but don't anyone mess with it, especially if you yourself don't believe in what's in the God box. How can I say I don't believe what's in the God box if someone replaces what's there?

Maybe we should take a look at some of the things people put in their God box. Maybe you have some of them in yours. What kind of god is in your box?

1. Is the god in your box one that picks sides in a war to help the selected side defeat their enemies? The Israelites certainly believed that was true. Today it may be the god that helps your team win on the basketball court or the football field. We have many examples of athletes paying homage to this god after a spectacular play on the sports field.
2. Does the god in your box have a special people or religion through whom and only through whom he works? Do you believe your religion is God's "true" religion? Are you involved with converting people to your view of God so they too can be a "chosen one"? Does that extend to believing your denomination is God's select denomination?
3. Does the god in your box intervene in nature? Is this god responsible for natural disasters, i.e., hurricanes and tornadoes, as well as good weather? Does this god cause disasters to teach people the error of their ways? Have you ever prayed for rain,

I BELIEVE IN GOD: WHAT DOES IT MEAN?

expecting this god to send it? If you pray for rain, do you then carry an umbrella?

4. Is the god in your box in control of your illness or your wellness? Is this god your protector from accidents or even death? Does this god provide you with travel mercies? In case that is a new term for you, does this god watch over you as you travel? Is how, where, and when you will die a foregone conclusion already set and known by this god? When you are gone, however your death took place, will those left behind say it was the will of this god?

5. Is the god in your box one who has a set of rules to which you must adhere to gain favor? Is this god one who will punish the evildoer—those who don't follow the rules—and reward the righteous—those who follow the rules? Is your view on this one a big motivator of your behavior? Do you ever have questions about who interprets the rules from this god?

6. Can the god in your box be controlled through the fervent use of prayer—if your faith is strong enough? If you have many people praying for you rather than just a few, does the volume of prayers have a greater influence on this god? If this god can't be influenced, is it because of your sinful nature, or because you don't have enough prayers or enough faith?

7. Is the god in your box one that demands worship as a king demands subservience? Do you consider yourself to be totally unworthy in the eyes of this god? Do you regularly let this god know just how unworthy you are?

8. Does the god in your box demand acceptance of certain "correct beliefs" if you are to gain this god's acceptance? Who has the authorization to determine these "correct beliefs"? Are there consequences from this god if those "correct beliefs" are not accepted?

9. Does the god in your box reside somewhere above the sky in a realm called heaven? Has this god provided you with a clear picture of what this heaven looks like? Do you believe you will

join this god there someday? Does this god tell you who to expect will be there with you?
10. How does the god in your box deal with evil? Is this god more powerful? If this god is more powerful than evil, then why does this god allow evil? Is it possible this god may even cause or at least allow evil? If this god allows evil, why?

If the god in your God box fits some of the descriptions above, welcome to mainline Christianity. The god described above is still the prevalent view of God that most Christians carry around in their God box. This God is still the primary object and substance of the faith of the Christian Church. There are other things that could be in your God box, but most of them will be related to the items listed above. Even those who have "I don't believe in God" boxes use the above criteria to determine the contents of their box.

Who or what is God? Some of you will already be after me because of my first sentence inferring that God may be a "what" rather than a "who." The "what" can be a presence rather than a personality. Throughout the centuries and in all religions, humans have created God in their image. A philosopher of the eighteenth century, Ludwig Feuerbach, made the claim humans create a god to meet their perceived image of God. It is no more than a projection of a being who could meet their needs of security and desires. This image has definitely been one with personality. The God image through the ages has been remarkably similar to the people who hold to that image, regardless of the religious group. There is an old saying, "If horses had gods, they would look and act remarkably like horses."

In my first and only civilian pastorate, I was teaching a Sunday school class on Genesis 1. I asked what it means to say we are made in the image of God. One man answered: "An image is a small replica of the real thing. Therefore, God looks like us, only much bigger." Most of you probably think the image of God looking like us only bigger is humorous, and it is. What is sad is that conceptually many images people have about their God are at about that level. God is

I BELIEVE IN GOD: WHAT DOES IT MEAN?

also probably an older male with a white beard. He would look like Michelangelo's painting of God on the ceiling of the Sistine Chapel in the Vatican. The title of one of Elvis Presley's songs probably captures many people's concepts of God more accurately than we may want to believe. The title is: "I Believe in the Man in the Sky." Another song from years ago contains the line, "Have you talked to the man upstairs…" These two songs illustrate the *where* of God in most people's minds, if not the *who* or *what*.

God is a word used by humans to explain an idea that is basically unexplainable because it goes beyond human ability to define. God is an infinite rather than a finite concept. How can you explain the infinite with finite words? Language is not equipped to deal with a concept that is greater than any logic or idea we may fabricate. We still try, and we do it by calling the concept "God." Anselm, an eleventh century theologian and Bishop of Canterbury, is said to have referred to God as that which nothing greater than can be conceived.

I like to think that God is love. Most Christians would probably say they believe God is love. At the same time it is amazing the bizarre acts of the past that Christians have attributed to this God of love. Some of God's atrocities look very much like the atrocities human beings have inflicted on each other. In the Old Testament, the Jewish God was assumed to hate anyone the Jewish people hated, and vice versa. Many people died because the Jewish people sincerely believed God told them to exterminate certain peoples. Ever hear of the Holocaust? At least God wasn't listed as the one who gave the order. Our forefathers in the Western world pursued colonial expansion in the seventeenth, eighteenth, and nineteenth centuries. There were those who believed this colonization of primitive tribes and peoples was actually the will of God. The heathen had to be Christianized—westernizing was also included.

The bloodiest war involving the United States was the Civil War. There were members from the same family on opposite sides. It is generally considered to be a war about slavery. There were Christians who believed God had willed the black man to be subservient to others. Not

GOD IN A BOX

everyone agreed with that viewpoint, and we had a war. How many thousands were killed protecting what God had wrought? But what had God wrought? Was he for or against slavery? This is a good example of humans creating God in their own image and believing what they believe is what God believes.

St. Francis of Assisi, St. Thomas Aquinas, Martin Luther, John Calvin, and John Wesley are a few of the names familiar in the history of Christianity. God probably was defined and acted in accordance with their individual concepts of God. The qualities attributed to God are very often human qualities expanded beyond the human limitations of the person or persons describing them. We love; God can love better. We hate, and God can be even more hateful. We can be vengeful, but nothing compared to the vengeance of God. We could go on, but I think the point has been made. People do add a few attributes to that, to make sure God is greater than we are. God is all-knowing of both past and future, God is all-powerful, and God is present everywhere at once. These concepts have to be added on, or else what good is the man in the sky or upstairs? How can he bail us out if he doesn't have those attributes?

I believe it is important what kind of God we have in our God box. What we see could be a purely academic vision. It is important how we experience God in our daily lives rather than what we see in the box. I firmly believe it can affect the credibility of Christianity in particular (because I am a Christian) and religion in general. The way we perceive God can make God seem real or even unreal. The way we see God can make God seem real to us, but unreal to others. Those thoughts can also make God seem near to us or very far away.

There is a direct correlation between one's idea of God in the God box and how one decides what it means to follow this God. Since I consider myself to be a Christian, my view of God will be influenced by Christian thought. Is following God focused on this life or the life hereafter? Something I heard many years ago speaks to that. "Some people are completely caught up with the idea of pie-in-the-sky by and by. They are so heavenly minded they are no earthly good." I have

I BELIEVE IN GOD: WHAT DOES IT MEAN?

certainly seen that in action and maybe you have as well.

I read about a poll taken to determine why people were Christian. Of those interviewed, a large majority said one of the main reasons they were Christian was to make sure they made it to heaven. The percentage isn't as important as to what it points. There are many people who are Christians to pursue a type of eternal security. If pursued, I'm sure the backside of that answer may have been to keep from going to hell, which in their mind might be a form of fire insurance. Unfortunately, the fear of hell seems to be more of a motivator for religious behavior than love of God.

Again, I ask someone to give me a good description of heaven. Do you know anyone who has been there and returned with a firsthand report? Now the fundamentalists will be on my case for sure.

Is the Christian life about holding certain "correct beliefs"—to get you into heaven and keep you out of hell—or is it more about a life being transformed through following the teachings of Jesus? Is the Christian life a matter of behavior or a matter of belief—or possibly a mixture of both? When I was growing up I heard people talk the talk in church on Sunday but didn't appear to walk the walk during the week. That obvious discrepancy between walk and talk almost kept me from becoming a minister. It wasn't until years later that I fully grasped the concept that what was important to them were one's "correct beliefs." If those were on target, your behavior could be overlooked because you were a believer. These "correct beliefs" could constitute a long list. The five fundamentals I listed earlier would certainly be on the list. In my upbringing, the inerrant Bible was a must. The virgin birth would have also had a high priority. It was also extremely important and necessary to believe in a literal heaven and a literal hell. The preachers and evangelists needed hell to scare people into being Christian. There is nothing better than a hellfire sermon to scare the hell out of the listener. Maybe I should rephrase that: scaring the listener out of hell. Remember the majority mentioned above? Heaven was important. You needed to give people something to look forward to in order to make it worthwhile to be a Christian.

GOD IN A BOX

Does the Christian life mean being preoccupied with pie-in-the-sky, or being involved in making Earth a better place? Does being a Christian translate to emphasizing "correct beliefs" and who is in and who is out, or should the emphasis be on compassion for others and inclusion? I guess the bottom line for me is whether the Christian life is more about "correct beliefs" or more about transformed relationships. I stand in the camp of transformed relationships.

I think I got off track. I go back now to Christian ideas of God. I'm sure there are many ideas out there in people's God boxes. I'm going to limit my discussion to three ideas. I believe all of these are seen in the Christian tradition. There are those who would disagree with me, and that's okay. I'm not out to prove a point, but to give brief explanations of these ideas. I should also state it is possible for some overlap in a person's thinking.

Our starting place is the idea of God as a supernatural deity who exits "out there" somewhere. It is often referred to as supernatural theism. I think it is safe to say some version of this God idea is in more God boxes than any other idea. If we look at the history of the Christian religion, we would see that it is in the framework of supernatural theism that most Christians have thought about God. It is the idea still held by the majority of those who call themselves Christian. It is the idea I grew up with and held to very stubbornly for many years. I also need to say when an atheist proclaims to not believe in God, this is most likely the idea of God in which the atheist doesn't believe.

Basically, this idea puts God out there—or up there—somewhat separated from the real world. This God created the world—and we should include the entire universe—eons ago. The literalists would say in the range of 6,000 years ago. This is in line with the chronology of creation given by Bishop James Ussher (1581–1656). Bishop Ussher was an Irish theologian and scholar. He had an extremely large collection of books. Some even credited him with at one time having the most extensive collection of books in Western Europe. This large collection became a donation to Trinity College, Dublin, a college his uncle James Ussher helped establish. Even though we might question

I BELIEVE IN GOD: WHAT DOES IT MEAN?

the validity of his studies and conclusions, in his day he was seen as a defender of learning. He was a proponent of the Irish Protestant faith, and in 1625 he was appointed Archbishop of Armagh.

His chronology of creation is his most well-known work. Most literalists are aware of the chronology, even if they are not aware of who designed it or how. Bishop Ussher took the book of Genesis and added up all the years in the "begats." What a tedious job that must have been. Have you ever tried just to read them? This led to his conclusion that the universe was created in the year 4004 BC, on October 23. Not to be outdone, there were others who continued the research and pinpointed the time as exactly 9 a.m., London time. This was also considered to have been midnight in the Garden of Eden. This chronology appeared in the margins of many editions of the Authorized Version of the Bible, otherwise known as the King James Version, in the nineteenth century. This miscalculation by this learned bishop has been used by generations since as "proof" of the error of believing in evolution, molecular biology, astrophysics, and any other scientific endeavors in the twentieth and twenty-first centuries that would contradict that theory. We have no idea how Bishop Ussher would see the time line of creation proposed by modern science. If he was truly a scholar, I'm sure he would at least take a look at the proof presented. After all, there is much information available that was unknown when he did his research.

We got off on a real rabbit chase by mentioning a God up there who created the universe. He still keeps an eye on his creation, and from time to time may intervene in what happens to it and to those who live in it. I use "he" because this idea does picture a masculine God. That "he" is believed to intervene, if he so desires, gives this God a strong security-producing role. This intervention can be called upon if you pray hard enough, worship in the right manner, have enough faith, and keep the faith in the approved manner by having the "correct beliefs." This kind of thinking has actually become an obstacle to faith. For some people, this becomes an obstacle to belief in any god. God is perceived as a doubtful reality, and he is seen as very far away,

GOD IN A BOX

if he exists at all.

Sigmund Freud, in his book *The Future of an Illusion*, 1927, made the claim that theistic religion grew out of the trauma of self-consciousness. It states that at one point in time, there was no concept of self. Neither was there any concept that someday the self would cease to exist.

Somewhere along the way self-consciousness introduced itself to human beings. These beings, now self-consciousness, were very frightened by the world in which they existed. They wanted to find meaning in things happening to them and around them and developed a belief that there were spirit beings that inhabited things. These were unseen forces that affected their lives. Some believed beings of some type inhabited everything around them. It was not too much of a reach to start calling these beings "gods." These gods were in control of all that happened. There were many gods, some belonging to different tribes, and some actually confined to particular areas or events. For example, there could be a god of the mountain as well as a god of thunder and lightning. Many people recognized these gods, even if it was not the god they worshipped.

Even though they accepted there were many gods, the Hebrew people came to believe their one supernatural theistic being was greater than any of the other gods. It was this god being that explained all that was beyond human understanding. This supernatural theistic God became humankind's ally in the fight for survival in a world in which the deck was stacked against them. It was in this process that humankind hoped to find a reason for existence and some purpose in life. Freud would say theism came about as a human coping device, created by humankind, now a self-conscious being, as a way to deal with the anxiety that comes with self-consciousness. It sounds reasonable to me. You decide.

All creatures are aware of the forces of nature around them—storms, lightning, hurricanes, fire, thunder, earthquakes, or any other frightening phenomena. But what self-consciousness brought to humankind was the knowledge that death one day was the ultimate end. Being

I BELIEVE IN GOD: WHAT DOES IT MEAN?

born is the beginning of a terminal existence. It is the starting point of a journey to death. No one gets out of this world alive. Humans are the only creatures who know this to be true. Knowing death waits creates anxiety. The threat of non-being is difficult to grasp. The God of supernatural theism was perceived as the protector of humankind. The transcendence of God becomes an important emphasis. Simply stated, this means God was seen as being beyond any limits and was beyond human experience and knowledge. He was beyond anything finite, and he was beyond the universe and material existence. Getting on God's good side would appear to be to your advantage. Maybe you could get God to intervene when times were scary and tough. Maybe God could help you delay the inevitable end—death. This is certainly the God you wanted in your box!

It is my belief that supernatural theism can provide an easy path to skepticism at the least and atheism at the extreme. I probably should add another spinoff: apathy toward the Christian faith. Apathy might very well be the one most prevalent in our society today.

There is another idea about God which has been out there for a while and may still exist is some God boxes. However, it is not very prevalent in our present age. The idea is called deism. Deism was strong during the Age of Enlightenment (eighteenth century). I mention it because it probably was the God idea held by many of the founders of America. This is to the consternation of those who want to claim we are a Christian nation and always have been. This creates a problem for them, because many do not believe deists should be considered truly Christian. Just another case of "If you don't believe like I do, you are wrong." One of the prime examples of a follower of deism was Thomas Jefferson. There are many books available about him and by him. He was a prolific writer and put down many of his religious thoughts. About God, Jefferson said, "It does me no injury for my neighbor to say there are twenty gods, or no god. It neither picks my pocket nor breaks my leg." He even put together his own version of the New Testament. It's an interesting book to read and I recommend it.

The deist believes God created the world, put things in motion, and now it's on its own. It could be likened to an artist and the artist's art. This also is sometimes illustrated by using the analogy of a watchmaker. A watchmaker makes a watch, and after it is made, it is on its own. The maker doesn't intervene in the works. Some people would say if it has a main spring, it needs to be wound up regularly, and if damaged, it needs repaired. Consider the watch a perpetual watch. Once made, it is put on its own. Sort of like the universe. The deist God does not intervene in the laws of the universe he created any more than the watchmaker interferes with the works of the watch he has made. The deist does emphasize morality, but rational thinking and reason are better guides to developing religious thought and morality than revelation. Miracles are not a part of deists' beliefs.

The last idea I want to deal with is panentheism—not *pantheism*. There are probably not very many God boxes holding this, but I think it is growing in popularity. Simply put, pantheism is God is everything and everything is God, which could be interpreted to mean that God is not a distinct being but is synonymous with the universe. Panentheism is a God idea in which God is a very essential part of nature, but also extends beyond it. In panentheism God is seen as the infinite eternal force in the universe, and is greater than the universe. This idea is receiving more acceptance among Christians as an alternative to supernatural theism. This idea is one that fits very well with the image of God as ground of being, discussed later in this chapter.

God is the encompassing spirit. This concept stresses God's active presence in the universe, not just a supernatural being somewhere out there. This has the effect of avoiding an isolation of God from the world. Instead, God and the world are interrelated, with God being in the world and the world being in God. God is a dimension of reality all around us; he is not somewhere else, like up there, but right here. We should also say if God is everywhere, it means God becomes a dimension of our own being. Seeing God as a dimension of our own being is very difficult for some to accept. It doesn't mean each of us is a god. Panentheism holds to the immanence (he's all around us) of God and the transcendence (he also goes beyond us) of God. Panentheism as an idea about God is still foreign to the thinking of most Christians. This is primarily due to the many centuries of influence from the idea of supernatural theism.

There are critics who claim panentheism is not biblical. I'm not trying to turn this into a proof texting exercise, but I will mention a few scriptures supporting the idea of panentheism. In Isaiah 6:3, *"...the whole earth is full of God's glory."* Psalm 19:1, *"The heavens are telling the glory of God; and the firmament proclaims his handiwork."* Psalm 139:7, *"Where can I go from your spirit? Or where can I flee from your presence?"* John 17:3, *"And this is eternal life, that they may know you, the only true God and Jesus Christ whom you have sent."* This also tells me eternal life is to be seen as a present reality, not a future hope. We are living eternal life in the present because we know God in the present. We read in Acts 17:27-28, *"...so that they would search for God and perhaps grope for him and find him—though indeed he is not far from each one of us. For 'In him we live and move and have our being'..."*

People talk about experiences that to them seem to be sacred. If it is true that the sacred—God—can be experienced, then it would appear that God is not just out there, but also right here. As they further describe these experiences, they indicate that they don't just cause a feeling, but a knowing. They describe an awareness of a whole different layer of reality, of knowing something much beyond just a feeling. Those we consider as having been stalwarts in the three major monotheist religions of the world seem to have had such experiences—Moses, Muhammad, and Jesus. These episodes can be described as mystical experiences that involve a level of consciousness in which the person is vividly aware of the presence of God.

It is not unusual to have a person relate an experience of a higher power that led to a transformed and loving perception of people and the world. Discovering this higher power is certainly one of the steps in an alcoholic becoming a recovering alcoholic. To me, this suggests a God encountered right here, right now. Experiences people relate as in some way being equated with a religious experience suggest God is an element of experience, not simply an article of faith in which to believe.

GOD IN A BOX

Whatever your idea of God, remember that God cannot be described or defined. Whatever your God box might include, God is more. There have been books written about the indescribable God. Lao-tzu, a Chinese philosopher from 2,500 years ago, is considered to be the founder of Taoism. He said, "The Tao that can be named is not the eternal Tao." Replace the word "Tao" with the word "God." St. Augustine said, "…when you begin to experience God you realize that what you are experiencing you cannot be put into words." The Jewish faith has a prohibition against graven images of God. This is making the same point; God cannot be named or defined, only experienced.

The bottom line is that all of our attempts to define and explain God are really attempts to describe and define the indescribable. Ideas about God are just those—ideas. Attempted conceptualization of God is trying to put God in a box. God does not fit in a box! The God in whom I live and move and have my being is beyond any box or idea! At the same time, we must not forget that because something is indescribable, it does not mean it isn't real or present. Carl Jung, a Swiss psychiatrist and founder of the school of analytical psychology, said, "Bidden or not bidden, God is present."

If God is generalized as a being out there, it does influence how you live your religious faith. This can be interpreted to mean God is definitely not here. The Christian life may be interpreted as essentially about beliefs and requirements. It can be seen as believing in a supernatural being "out there," in order to achieve the high goal of an afterlife in the sweet by and by. The Christian life should be about how we live relationally with God right now, right here. You can proclaim at an intellectual level to hold to a set of beliefs without those beliefs having much effect on your behavior. You cannot encounter the God who is indescribable without entering into a manner of living that can and will change your life. For the fundamentalist, this may be what is called a conversion experience. However, it is not just a matter of walking down the aisle or raising your hand and saying "I believe" and conversion is instantaneous. It is more an issue of entering into a process in which a growing understanding of the compassion of God impacts

I BELIEVE IN GOD: WHAT DOES IT MEAN?

how you the individual live out God's compassion.

There are those, generally of a fundamentalist approach, who are very willing to tell you all about God, listing all his good attributes—and his not-so-good attributes. Any attempt at a logical discussion with such a person is rather futile. They seem to have a mission in life motivating them to make sure you know all there is to know about God—as they see God in their box—and it is the correct vision. They are not interested in conversation; they are more interested in conversion—yours! They have the same mindset as the little boy drawing a picture and asked by his mother, "Son, what are you drawing?" The little boy answered, "I'm drawing a picture of God." "But son," the mother responded, "no one knows what God looks like." The little boy responded, "They will when I get through!"

I want to move on to images people have of God. It is important to go beyond ideas. We need to look at more specific images people apply to fill out their ideas about the God in their box. Images provide attributes that are more tangible, visible, and metaphorical ways in which you may perceive of God or speak about God. These images also have an influence on how you live your religious faith. If people think one of God's attributes is being a militant, they may become militants. This could be why people joined a Christian Crusade. It might also explain why a person could become a Muslim jihadist suicide bomber. Is it possible that a person would join an apocalyptically oriented militia for the same reason? Certainly there are stories in the Old Testament that support a militant God. Didn't he lead the Israelites to many victories over their enemies?

Those who see God as compassionate are certainly more prone to be compassionate than those who hold the militant image. It is difficult for me to imagine a militant as being very compassionate. From time to time I hear people (often televangelists but not limited to them) stating how angry God is at the world. They also like to point out how God is going to get even. I saw a bumper sticker that proclaimed, "Jesus is coming back and he is pi_ _ed!" They even point to disasters as being caused by God to teach a lesson to a wayward individual, people, or nation. They seem to portray a lot of anger at the world but not much compassion.

When we look at scripture we can see many metaphors depicting biblical images of God. These are images based on human experiences of God. Remember earlier, I said humans create God in their own image. I believe these metaphors support that concept. It is important to point out that the main characteristic of metaphor is comparison. This simply means something is described as something else. God is monarch, lord, militant, judge, or lawgiver, all of which seem to be in the category of governing, authority, and enforcement. God is also creator, shepherd, healer, father, mother, lover, and friend. God is also described using nature and inanimate objects. He is eagle, lion, bear, fire, light, cloud, wind, breath, rock, fortress, and shield.

God is described using these various terms. It stands to reason that God is not literally these things—just *like* them. All of these are again an attempt to define or put God in a box of humans' making. Because that is impossible, the language we use about God must be metaphorical.

This is another of those times when something can be true even if not factual. If I say my wife is a beautiful rose, it does not mean she is literally a rose. She is *like* a rose—she is beautiful, brings joy, and brightens up a room. Notice that I likened her to more than one thing about a rose. Roses also have thorns, but I didn't use that in the metaphor. This is generally true about metaphors; there can be more than one application. That is why it is difficult to translate a metaphoric association to just one literal statement.

Now let's look at some examples. The word "king" appears in both the Old Testament and the New Testament. We have to remember that in the New Testament the word "king" is also applied to Jesus. What does the word mean as applied to God? My image of a king is greatly influenced by fictional and historical works I have read. When I think of attributes of a king I see several things. A king is surrounded by grandeur, majesty, and glory. He appears as someone who has it all, power, authority, and he makes the rules and also enforces them. He

I BELIEVE IN GOD: WHAT DOES IT MEAN?

can also be compassionate or punitive. A good king is concerned about justice and protection of his subjects. To cap it all off, kings are male. God is also the good shepherd. Does this mean he is literally a shepherd with a flock of sheep? I don't think so. God is also referred to as father. Does this mean he is literally our father? I don't think so. These examples illustrate that a metaphor can be relational. When God is king, we are his subjects. When God is shepherd, we are his sheep. When God is father, we are his children. None of this is literal, but it speaks volumes metaphorically. Some of our Christian hymns also support a king image of God. For example, "O Worship the King." This hymn provides a positive portrayal of God. It also suggests what we should be doing and what God will do for us.

I want to spend some more time with the metaphorical image of God as king or monarch. I chose this image because I think it has had a place of prominence in people's view of God since Constantine converted to Christianity in 312 CE. Constantine was also the one who issued the Edict of Milan, legalizing Christian worship throughout the Roman Empire (No, he wasn't the one who made it the official religion of the Roman Empire). I believe this image of God is one of the most prevalent images in the thinking of those who hold to a supernatural deity view of God. If you asked people their image of God, not many would say "king." I refer to this as a popular image because I believe if you asked people to describe the attributes of God, they would list attributes applicable to a king.

Several attributes belong to God in this image. Since kings are always male, God definitely has to be male. Like an earthly king, God holds the power of life and death, so he is all-powerful. He also makes the rules and enforces them. Our life in the after depends on how well we keep his laws in the here. Yes, I know grace has surpassed the law. Many who believe grace will bring salvation would still say making it to the heavenly place in the hereafter may not depend on keeping the laws, but will depend on having the "correct beliefs." Maybe I should change that to say that having the "correct beliefs" is the law! My study of history would indicate that many kings were distant from their subjects. Kings and subjects lived in two different worlds. And so it is for many, in this image of God, he is distant.

If you hold to the image God is king, how do you relate to such a being? In the minds of many, not easily. Kings have subjects, peasants who work their fields. That describes us; we are subjects and peasants. Because we are subjects, we owe the king loyalty and obedience. Because he makes and enforces the rules, it has an impact on how we behave. It impacts us because we have for years told ourselves we are only worthy to be peasants or servants. If we are disobedient to the king (God), it can bring dire consequences. There is punishment for disobeying a king's law; the king can be punitive. Translated religiously, sin is disobedience to God's law, so we deserve God's judgment and punishment for sin.

Not all kings should be thought of as being harsh. Many of them loved their subjects. When a loyal subject disobeyed a law, it created a dilemma. The law has been broken, the king demands justice, but he loves his subjects and also believes in mercy, so what to do? A good king finds a way for the lawbreaker to pay some type of compensation in lieu of the punishment. In the Old Testament sacrifices were the compensation offered to God to atone for disobedience. In the Christian version, the king's (God's) love is seen in Jesus. God as king is believed to require compensation because he is both lawgiver and judge, and disobedience requires punishment or compensation. The sacrifice of Jesus was the required compensation. Like a king who loves his subjects, God's love was so great he provided the sacrifice.

Having this kind of God in your God box does have an impact on how you live religiously. God is often viewed in this idea as a far, distant, and very powerful being definitely separated from the world. He is the authority figure "out there," or more probably "up there," and he is male. God perceived as male has real implications for the role of men and women. We already talked about some of the biblical views of women. There are churches that still believe it is the woman's place to play second fiddle to males. An example of this are churches that still refuse to allow women clergy. The Roman Catholic Church is certainly a prime example of this. They are not the only ones. There are many fundamentalist Protestant churches that still will not allow women clergy. That is not just because they claim Jesus had only male disciples—which is debatable—but is impacted by this monarchial view of God.

The God in a box as king has had a real impact on the role of men and women in society. I believe it has led to a societal hierarchy in which men are considered the dominant gender. Mary Daly, in her book *Beyond God the Father*, tells us when God is male, the male is God. The idea that God is male has been cited as providing reasonable justification that men should be dominant over women. All we need to do is look at our society, culturally, politically, and religiously. It becomes very clear the suppression of women is in evidence. How long did it take for women to get the right to vote? What is the percentage of women holding high political office? Don't forget to look at religious hierarchies. What's the percentage of clergy who are female? Even more evident is the low percentage of women in positions of bishops or comparable standing in churches that do not have bishops. This whole view just reemphasizes one more problem of supernatural theism—a God separate from the world who rules like a king—a male king.

If you hold this image of God in your God box, it will affect your behavior. We are less than perfect and we are sometimes disobedient subjects—whatever this disobedience to God is, it is called sin. Sin and guilt become central in this view of life and are possibly the most difficult problem faced by those holding this view. Roberta Bondi, in her book *Memories of God*, said: "Sin was what religion was about. ...Jesus was born in order to pay the price for our sin by suffering and dying on the cross." She goes on to say the way to get sins forgiven was to repent: "To feel really, really bad about what a sinful person you are." Stop and think about that for a moment. Many churches and clergy still promote this concept. How often is there a prayer of confession in the worship service? And how often do those prayers include a phrase about how unworthy we are and how bad we are? We confess to sins both known and unknown. This mindset confers upon the individual the idea that one must think of oneself as sinful, guilty, and unworthy of anything good. The acceptable way to feel really good about yourself in this situation is to feel really, really bad about yourself to show you are truly repentant.

Thinking this way may cause the voice of God to be confused with the voice of our own superego. The superego is where we keep our "oughts" and "shoulds." I say we need to quit going around "shoulding" on ourselves. Have you ever had someone shake a finger at you? What did it indicate? Generally it is accusatory and punitive. That's what the superego becomes. Life in this context is one of continually trying to live up to the oughts and shoulds standard. That makes it like living under the law. The superego becomes a little king in our head. It makes the laws and lets us know when we have broken them. Our God in a box certainly impacts what our superego tells us. The problem arises when we confuse what is the voice of God and what is the voice of our superego. The problem becomes exacerbated in that regardless of what we do, we are never good enough. To add to the mixture, we can claim this voice of God (or superego?) is God's will being spoken to us. We then justify our actions by saying this is what God desires us to do. We go about doing these things to prove we are good enough, but never really believe it. We continue to reach, but never achieve!

It becomes apparent that God in a box as king has had a significant impact on the Christian faith. Many who hold this God as king image still view the love of God as central. How they view this love in action would vary from individual to individual.

The God in a box that resonates best with me refers to God is spirit. It promotes a view of the Christian life in which relationships, transformation, and belonging are important aspects. Whereas the image of God is king to many translates into a physical image of God, God is spirit is seen as a nonphysical reality that permeates the universe and is also much more than the universe (remember panentheism?). It is also an image that defies complete description or definition. Even though it cannot be described, it can be felt.

We see the use of the title "spirit" throughout the scriptures. In

I BELIEVE IN GOD: WHAT DOES IT MEAN?

the Old Testament, it refers to God's presence in creation, and we definitely see it in the leading and history of Israel, the chosen people. In the New Testament it certainly is present in the life and ministry of Jesus and plays a prominent role in early Christianity. When we use the word "spirit" in any type of religious context, it generally has the connotation of sacred attached to it. Further, when we think of it in religious context, it almost always indicates the presence of divine activity. When we think of spirit, it has a strong association with God's presence in the world. The Hebrew word "ruach" in the Old Testament is translated as meaning "wind" and "breath." The implications of those meanings are many. Both wind and breath are invisible and yet quite real. At the same time, both can have an effect on what they come into contact with. For example, breathe on a cold winter window and see what happens—condensation appears. Another example is the destruction caused by a hurricane or tornado. You cannot see the wind, but you see the effects of the wind. If you stand in the wind, it completely surrounds you. So it is with spirit; it is all around you. God is the encompassing spirit within us and around us.

There are metaphors for God is spirit. For some people, these may call to mind physical images. My intent is for you to think in terms of characteristics, not physical presence. They are not exclusively male-related. For example, God can be seen as having characteristics of a mother. God is a mother, caring for and comforting her children. A mother is compassionate. God is also a father. God as father is a favorite usage with those who have God in a box as king. In the Bible, God as father often indicates a level of intimacy. This is readily seen in the New Testament where we see Jesus' use of "abba," an intimate form of "father." The image of a good father is one who stands by his children. A good father can be expected to be concerned about the welfare of his children. God is lover could also be a metaphor for God is spirit. Read the book of Hosea if you want an excellent portrayal of what it means to truly love. Want to read a good love story? Read the Song of Solomon. The story illustrates a type of mystical relationship existing between the lover (God) and the beloved (us).

GOD IN A BOX

In the New Testament we see the church referred to as the bride of Christ, Christ being the bridegroom. I like this as a great image for the divine-human relationship. You could also use this image to support the idea that the spirit image can be female or male. God is spirit can also be seen as a traveling companion. I'm not referring here to "travel mercies," when we pray that we will be protected by God in our travels. That takes us back to a supernatural theistic God who watches out for us. I'm referring to "companion" in the sense the presence of God is always with us. The story of the Emmaus Road in the New Testament tells a story of presence so strong the travelers thought Jesus was physically present with them (Luke 24:13-35).

If you have God in a box as spirit instead of king, what are the ramifications? God as being here is the emphasis, rather than God as being out there or far removed, which comes from the God as king image. One item I believe of critical importance is the use of both sexes metaphorically as God descriptors, not just masculine images as portrayed by the God as king image.

It is important to note that the image of God you have in your God box will always have a significant impact on how you live as a Christian. If you see God like a king, you probably visualize the king ordering creation to happen. Creation becomes an event past and over with long ago. If you see God through the spirit model, you will be more likely to see creation as an ongoing activity in which you are a participant. Creation is viewed as not limited to "in the beginning," but about what happens around you all the time, a continuing event in the present. For example, involvement in environmental concerns and actions is being a participant in the continuing creation. If you follow the king image, you may look at humans and say their main problem is they go around being disobedient. Disobedience is sin and so then they have to deal with the guilt. The king cannot tolerate such disobedience. Sin and guilt call for justice and punishment. We offend because we are unable to keep the law. The truth be told, sometimes we don't want to keep the law. What is the law we cannot keep? It is readily explained to us by fundamentalist practitioners, be they laypersons

I BELIEVE IN GOD: WHAT DOES IT MEAN?

or clergy. Now don't try to tell me "correct beliefs" are not considered law! These persons invariably hold to a strong king metaphor. The king makes the rules, enforces the rules, and metes out justice. You, the poor lowly sinner, can only cower in his (always male) presence and ask for forgiveness—even though you know you are unworthy to receive it.

If you follow the spirit model, you would say sin is being unfaithful by giving loyalty to something other than God. Many things can become a god (with little g) that can interfere with a relationship. The level of your relationships with others could also be seen as sin. Are you indifferent to the suffering of others? Even worse, have you inflicted some type of suffering on others you may see as being different from you—race, religion, place in society, nationality, or sexual preference? This could be a subtle one. Maybe all you do is consider yourself just a little bit better because of how you choose to live. This becomes not an issue of breaking the laws of God (correct beliefs), but an issue of not showing compassion, as God shows compassion as we see it revealed in the life of Jesus.

Some have probably already decided I am committing grievous sins for which I will have to answer in the hereafter. My sin would be not accepting the "correct beliefs." This would fit well with those who hold the God as king image. Sin is disobeying God's laws. Always be aware of who has made the decisions about what those laws entail. If I have been disobeying the fundamentalist concept of God's laws, I become a bona fide target.

Separation from God is certainly an ingredient in the spirit image of God. This separation may simply be an issue of being unaware of the presence of God. It may be an unawareness of the spiritual dimension of life. The answer to separation is reconciliation with the always present spirit. But what if the person is not even aware of the separation? It is not an issue of how bad we are because we sin readily and offend God. In a conversation with a friend, he told me he was not religious. I said that didn't bother me, but from what I knew about him, I thought he was a spiritual person. That comment seemed to catch him off guard. He said he didn't consider himself spiritual either. I explained

GOD IN A BOX

I believed everyone had a spiritual dimension, and it was a dimension active in all people. It was just that some people were unaware of any activity in that dimension. That is the way it is in terms of the presence of God. It is not that God is not present; it is again the issue of unawareness of that presence on the part of the individual. It might be there is no awareness of the presence of God because of the God image in the God box of the beholder—or should I say non-beholder? What they see or don't see depends on what they have in their God box. The Christian's task is not one of trying to convert the person who has no awareness of the spirit. The task is to show the spirit at work in one's own Christian's life. It means practicing forgiveness, compassion, love, and acceptance. Maybe your example will help someone else see the spiritual dimension and become aware a separation exists. Maybe they will become aware of a spiritual dimension they didn't even realize they had.

Is there any need for repentance in the spirit concept? Repentance is not done away with in the spirit concept. Repentance remains important. Repentance does not mean you look at the "correct beliefs" and suddenly say, "Now I believe." Repentance does not consist of you acknowledging how bad you are because of the evil things you have done—known and unknown. Repentance means getting your actions in accord with how God would have you act. This translates into acting compassionately, acting in a forgiving manner, and making your life be all it can be with the talents you have.

Does the spirit image allow us to escape judgment? Judgment can be a scary thought to some people. Bringing up the subject of judgment should make the fundamentalists say AMEN until they find out I'm not talking about the threat of an eternal fiery place of torment. Neither is it a place of eternal separation from God, whatever that might mean. Rather, judgment means everything we do has consequences, and not necessarily later. Earlier I mentioned separation from God. The judgment of making wrong choices can lead to estrangement and separation from God. The consequences can be we remain unsatisfied and unfulfilled. It may mean we do not feel the spirit of God within us.

I BELIEVE IN GOD: WHAT DOES IT MEAN?

The question becomes how we determine what are the wrong choices. I refer you back to the issue of sin. The wrong choices may be not having compassion. I also refer you to the reply of Jesus when asked about the great commandment. The first was to love God and the second was to love your neighbor as you love yourself. Of course, if you are into a kingly view of God and believe you are a wretched, bad, lowly sinner, undeserving of anything good, it might not be the best choice for you to love others as you love yourself. When I see the anger often directed by fundamentalists towards anyone who opposes them, compassion and love seem to be missing links. The letter of 1 John says it very well in 4:20-21, *"Those who say, 'I love God,' and hate their brothers or sisters, are liars; for those who do not love a brother or sister whom they have seen, cannot love God whom they have not seen. The commandment we have from him is this: those who love God must love their brothers and sisters also."* The feeble response sometimes given here is claiming these verses refer only to brothers and sisters in Christ. In other words only those who have "correct beliefs" are included in those we are to love.

So where does salvation enter the scenario? Does the need still exist? Most Christians, if asked, refer to salvation as securing a place in heaven after death—remember the majority response when asked why they were Christian? I like to think of it as something that happens in the present. It is directly related to our relationship with God as spirit. It is choosing to live life to the fullest. Remember, Jesus said he came that we might have life and have it more abundantly. Living in fear of hell doesn't sound like a very abundant life to me. I refer again to 1 John. In verses 4:18-19 he states, *"There is no fear in love, but perfect love casts out fear; for fear has to do with punishment, and whoever fears has not reached the perfection in love. We love because he first loved us."* Living a life of acceptance, compassion, and love seems to more accurately fit the God portrayed in the life of Jesus. A fundamentalist response could very well be to point out the verse refers to punishment, and people better be fearful if they don't have "correct beliefs"!

Earlier I stated I believed God is love (1 John 4:16b). I now state if that is true, then to say love is God would also be true. Well, maybe that is going a little too far. Perhaps it would be better to say love is of God. God becomes the life-giving spirit that challenges me to be the best I can be in following the example of Jesus. To do so is a tremendous challenge! Love must become the measure of all I do. I need to ask myself if my actions are based on what is most loving in the situation. That is influenced by my concept of self, my relationship with others, and is the bottom line in my understanding of God. I like the prophet Micah's proclamation, *"He has told you, O mortal, what is good; and what does the Lord require of you but to do justice, and to love kindness, and to walk humbly with your God?"* (Micah 6:8). I am very much aware that for some Christians walking humbly with God entails holding to "correct beliefs" and considering yourself unworthy of God's love. That is not my interpretation.

From the writings of Paul Tillich, I was first introduced to the idea of God as not a being but as being itself. Bishop John Shelby Spong's writing helped me to better understand the idea of God as "ground of being." One of the interpretations of the words to Moses from out of the burning bush is simply "I am!" That certainly sounds like being itself. The Jewish faith will not speak the name of God, based on the fact God cannot be named or explained. In Jewish thinking to name something is conceived as controlling that which is named. Remember Adam named the animals in the Genesis myth of creation, and he had dominion over them.

When discussing ideas about God contained in God boxes, I was basically talking about a few of the most prevalent concepts seen in today's world. I believe my concept of God puts me closer to the spirit model in my God box. Right at the top I see God is spirit. I like the words of John 4:24, *"God is spirit, and those who worship him must worship in spirit and truth."* This God is the spirit of all life in all creation. How do you put form to a spirit? This God is an infinite energy present in the entire universe. This God is the basis for the existence of all things in creation. This God is ultimate reality. This God is experienced as mystery that is absolutely too massive for us to ever probe its depths. The mystery is impossible to describe. This God is not some type of

I BELIEVE IN GOD: WHAT DOES IT MEAN?

super being who intervenes in the affairs of humankind. This God is the energy that becomes my motivation to intervene by loving, accepting, forgiving, and showing compassion. This God is all around you and even more important is in you. This God spirit is the very essence of who I am. This God spirit is within me, which motivates me to be the person I can and should be. This doesn't mean I achieve all I can be, but this God spirit does motivate me to keep trying. It also means I'm not condemned for not reaching my full potential. This God is the spirit that motivates me to live a life in which I strive to achieve the highest plateau in my ability to love, accept, and forgive. This God is the presence within me that encourages me to see others through eyes of compassion. This God is that which connects me to all life in the universe. This God is not a presence that fills me with fears of judgment and retribution should I not be holding to the "correct beliefs." To me this explains what is meant when God is referred to not as a being but as the ground of being! Bishop John A. T. Robinson, in his book *Honest to God*, summed it up very well with these words: "For the word 'God' denotes the ultimate depth of all our being, the creative ground and meaning of all our existence." I have heard it said it would be more appropriate to say God is more like a verb than a noun. I would interpret this to mean God is action, not object. I believe many Christians make God an object. He is that object out there we must worship. He is that object out there who can rescue us when needed. Change your thinking to God is love; love is action!

There is a short dialogue Galileo had with the priest Sagredo and recorded in *The Life of Galileo*, by Bertolt Brecht, and translated by John Willett:

"SAGREDO: So where is God?
GALILEO: I'm not a theologian. I'm a mathematician.
SAGREDO: First and foremost you're a human being. And I'm asking: where is God in your cosmography?
GALILEO: Within ourselves or nowhere."

I can sum it up by saying the God of supernatural theism does not exist for me. There is no man upstairs who will answer all our prayers.

GOD IN A BOX

It is extremely important to realize that the death of supernatural theism does not mean the death of God. Contrary to what the fundamentalist mindset would have you believe, the death of supernatural theism does not mean the birth of atheism. To the contrary, in my opinion, the belief in supernatural theism contributes to the cause of atheism. I do believe if we don't give people something to replace supernatural theism, the death of supernatural theism will more likely lead to the birth of apathy. I believe that process is already under way. The outcome of the death of supernatural theism is discovering a God reality that is more personal and present.

The death of supernatural theism results in a freedom from "shoulds," "oughts," and "correct beliefs." It brings a challenge to live a life more in tune with how Jesus lived his life, showing compassion and loving more readily, including loving the unlovable. The beauty of a life lived in this manner is life becoming motivated by "I want to," rather than "I have to" or "I'm afraid not to." I want to because the God within me frees me to live not in fear of an angry, wrathful, and punitive God but in the spirit of the God portrayed in the life of Jesus. I do not live to figure out how best to please this God in order to receive his protection and good graces. I live to make every day a day in which my life can say God is love and love is God. In all of this, I can really do nothing more than describe my own experiences with this ground of being in my life. It is life focused on the here rather than the after! God is infinite but we are finite. When the infinite one becomes a part of my finiteness, God is truly present. Is it possible the divine we seek is this infinite dimension of our finite being? What did Luke record Paul as saying in Acts 17:28? *"For in him we live and move and have our being..."* Nothing else needs to be said. What is the god in your God box? You decide.

4

WHO IS JESUS?

At the outset, I want to make it clear Jesus was not the first Christian, nor did he come to establish the Christian faith. Jesus was never a Christian! Jesus was an adult male who practiced the Jewish faith. It is also important to keep in mind much of what has been said and written about Jesus cannot be proven to be historical. There is some mention of Jesus in historical documents of the first century. I personally believe Jesus was a person of history. I do not believe the gospels are historical accounts about this Jesus of history. The gospels are not biographies. So right away I have some people shaking their heads and wondering what is wrong with me. I can turn that around and ask, "What is wrong with you?" Are you a member of the church in which Caleb was raised? As we move on, please think about what view of Jesus you have in your God box.

Credible New Testament scholars all agree that the gospels are not historical or eyewitness accounts about Jesus. You may disagree with me because you know some smart person or have read some book that has laid out the proof that the Jesus of the gospels is based on eyewitness accounts. Being smart should not be confused with being a credible New Testament scholar.

I have mentioned credible scholarship before. Let me expand on how to differentiate a credible scholar from one I would not consider credible. A credible New Testament scholar is intelligent, explores the text and any information that can be gleaned such as date of writing, language in which written, authorship, circumstances under which written, plus any other available documents. Based on study, a decision is made about the particular writing. There are no preconceived notions about what should be found. A non-credible New Testament scholar may be intelligent and use the same materials, but enters the study with a bias or preconceived idea about what will be found. Conclusions are then based on proving the bias rather than letting the research lead where it will. One of the popular quotes from Albert Einstein is, "A man should look for what is, and not what he thinks should be." I believe Albert Einstein would pass as a credible scholar. He was not a scholar in the field of New Testament research, but I believe his statement is good for any field of research. All this may be considered a rather skimpy explanation of differences, but I think it is basically solid and shows the difference.

Most people tend to read the gospels, and for that matter the entire Bible, devotionally, not critically. That should not be a surprise, as most of us were raised to see the Bible as devotional material. It was used in devotions and in sermons. Even when studied in a Sunday school class or Bible study, it was studied devotionally, not critically. By devotional study, I mean the focus is more on what it means in the life of the learners. I know I read it that way for years. I should add there might have been some focus on whether it really happened. For many people in devotional study, whatever the scripture is describing, it is accepted as a literal event. There is little focus on historical accuracy, when written, and questions of authorship. Because of the sequence of books in the New Testament, there is also a tendency to accept the order in which they appear as the order in which they were written. That is far from the truth. The first New Testament book written that refers to Jesus was the epistle 1 Thessalonians, written by Paul in the early 50s CE. All the generally agreed-upon authentic writings of Paul are believed to have been written before any of the gospels were written. I say authentic because there are some books attributed to Paul

WHO IS JESUS?

most scholars agree were written after his death. Since I have raised the issue, I will list the two categories here, although that is not the thrust of this chapter. It is important to know that anything Paul wrote about Jesus was written earlier than the gospels. Always keep that in mind when reading the New Testament. Most scholars agree that Paul wrote 1 Thessalonians, Galatians, 1 and 2 Corinthians, Romans, Philemon, and Philippians. The six others attributed to Paul, but believed to have been written within ten years after his death (65-75 CE), are 2 Thessalonians, Colossians, Ephesians, 1 and 2 Timothy, and Titus. It is beyond the scope of this chapter to go into the reasons why most scholars make the above distinctions. If you are really interested in pursuing that subject, there are books available with explanations.

So let me start again. The gospels were not written as biographies by eyewitnesses. They were written by men who interpreted the meaning of Jesus for particular times, places, and people. Matthew in particular wrote by looking back into the Old Testament and retelling stories of stalwarts of the Jewish faith and applying those stories to Jesus. This is different from claiming the sayings of the Old Testament prophesied the coming of Jesus. It is saying that the gospel writers took stories of the Old Testament and retold them using Jesus as the main character.

An example of the non-history of the gospels can be found by simply taking a look at the genealogies presented in Matthew and Luke. If these were historical accounts and an accurate part of a biography of Jesus, they should read the same. They don't. In Matthew it goes back to Abraham, in Luke it goes back to Adam. There are four women listed in Matthew's genealogy account. Check out Joseph's genealogy back to his great-grandfather. It is different. Makes you wonder where God's hand was when these genealogies were written, especially if God dictated and man wrote. And no, they cannot be reconciled by saying Matthew's genealogy is Joseph's side of the family and Luke is Mary's side of the family. In Luke 3:23, Luke states rather explicitly the line is that of Joseph. Another minor problem here is trying to trace the ancestry of Jesus back to King David by use of the genealogies. Remember, Jesus was to come from the lineage of David, and at the end of each genealogy is the father of Jesus, Joseph. If Mary was a virgin, and the bloodlines were passed down through the father, how could Jesus be from the lineage of David? There are many more discrepancies in the gospels if we try to read them as biographies. If you believe there are no discrepancies, I will never convince you. If you already accept there are discrepancies, I don't need to convince you.

Many people believe Matthew was the first gospel written about Jesus because it appears first in the New Testament. Not so, because Mark was the first gospel written about Jesus, somewhere around 70 CE. Remember, this would be years after Paul had died, and I have already pointed out that Paul authored the first recorded New Testament writings we have referring to Jesus. Next were probably Matthew and then Luke and finally John. Matthew and Luke leaned heavily on Mark and embellished what Mark had written. One example is the virgin birth. Mark contains no reference to a virgin birth. Matthew and Luke added that. They don't agree on what events surrounded the birth of Jesus. I will discuss this more later in the chapter. They do agree that Jesus was born of a virgin and she was pledged to be married to Joseph. The Christmas pageantry each year is a combined reading of Matthew and Luke and certainly should not be considered as historical, which may make some readers hysterical. Each gospel is an interpretation of Jesus. Does this mean they were not telling the truth? Their goal was to interpret the meaning of the life of Jesus to those who followed him, not portray a historical snapshot of his life. I remind you again that something can be metaphorically true, even if not literally true.

We also need to be aware the four gospels included in the canon of the New Testament were not the only gospels written about Jesus. One in particular had a significant impact on the writings of Matthew and Luke. We don't even have a copy of it. So how do we know it exists? We know by a close reading of Matthew and Luke. There are the same stories in each that did not come from Mark but seem to come from some other same source. This source is often called the Q document, from the German word "*Quelle*," which means source. Most biblical scholars consider this source to be a lost gospel to which Matthew and

Luke had access but was lost somewhere along the way and no copies are known to exist.

The Gospel of Thomas is not the only other writing found referring to Jesus, but it is one scholars give a lot of credibility. It is also one that has been helpful in researching more about the life and teachings of Jesus. This gospel was found near Nag Hammadi, Egypt, in December 1945. It is basically a collection of the sayings attributed to Jesus. What is interesting about it is the absence of any stories of miracles, the crucifixion, or the resurrection. It has been given enough attention to be included in a book by members of the Jesus Seminar with the title, *The Five Gospels*.

I have said I believe Jesus is a person of history. But if the gospels are not biographical, how do we find the true historical Jesus? Biblical scholars have been working on that one for years. A classic in the field is Albert Schweitzer's *The Quest of the Historical Jesus*. After all is said and done, he says we may never be able to identify the true historical Jesus. That should not deter us from searching to find out all we can about Jesus. Neither should that take away from the impact the life of Jesus has had on the lives of millions of people throughout the centuries. Schweitzer further says it is in following, not in believing, we are able to grasp who Jesus really is. That was of extreme significance in Schweitzer's life. He is one of the greatest, if not the greatest, Christian of the twentieth century. He truly followed Jesus. Read about his work in his free medical clinic in Lambarene. His beliefs about Jesus would not pass the test of "correct beliefs," but his actions would certainly witness to a life transformed as a follower of Jesus. Too mention just a few things, he did not believe in miracles, a resuscitated bodily resurrection, the virgin birth or a second coming sometime at the end of time. What I think is a real contribution is that Schweitzer's book may have provided the motivation for continuing the search for the historical Jesus.

It is helpful to take a look at what we know about the society at the time Jesus lived. There was very definitely an upper class and a lower class. From what we know historically about the first century, we can assume the upper class was very much a minority in numbers. Even though small in number, they exerted powerful control over the lower class. We could classify it as a society of the haves and the have-nots in an extreme sense. The upper class included those who governed, were a small percentage of the population, and owned a lot of the land. The priests were included in the upper class and owned some of the land. Technically, they were not allowed to own land. They got around it by claiming what they were prohibited from doing was working the land—they had others work it for them. Those who worked for the governing class and priests were included in the upper class. The best way to become a part of the upper class was to be born into it. However, there were merchants who may have started in the lower class and eventually worked their way up the social ladder to the upper class. A difficult task but doable.

The lower class had several groupings. Included here were the peasants who were by far the largest majority of the population. They were able to farm land they owned, and if allowed to keep their crops would have been much better off. The problem was most of their crops went to support the upper classes. The approximately one-third that they were allowed to keep kept them living at a bare subsistence level. This was in a good year. If drought or some other calamity forced them to give up their land, they ended up as a type of sharecropper or worse. Members of the peasant class had a life expectancy of approximately thirty years. Artisans, who were not a large percentage of the population, were considered lower than peasants. This was another place a peasant who lost land might end up. As a carpenter, Jesus would have been categorized in this class. His living would have been one of bare subsistence.

There was still a class lower than the artisans. Included in this group were those whose occupation would have the rest of society view them as outcasts. In this group you would find beggars, day laborers, criminals, and slaves. Most of those in the lower class were considered expendable, and this outcast group was considered the most expendable of all.

An age of literacy it was not. During the time of Jesus, the illiteracy rate has been estimated to be as high as 95-97 percent. This raises the real possibility Jesus was also illiterate. Some of you will immediately want to remind me of the story of the twelve-year-old Jesus astounding the scholars at the temple. We don't know if it is historical or not. Jesus may have had some knowledge of Hebrew, but it doesn't say they were amazed by his ability to read and write. Rather, they were amazed by his answers and understanding. He may have been taught in a synagogue school, but we simply don't know. It is even possible there was no synagogue in the small village where Jesus lived. Another one of the things we just don't know.

The affluent and powerful ruled this society and oppressed everyone under them. This is often referred to as a domination system when one class rules all others. The powerful included those who were in political power. This type of society was definitely politically oppressive. It imposed a heavy burden on peasants to support the upper class. These societies were certainly economically exploitive of those not in power. Wars were also a characteristic of this type of society. The governing classes had armies to defend their holdings, or if the occasion arose, attempt to increase their holdings.

The social and cultural world in which we live certainly shapes us as individuals. Jesus was shaped by the oppressive system under which he grew up and lived. Not only was there political oppression, but there was also a system of religious oppression. The top religious authorities were often in league with the political powers to help keep the masses under control. Remember, it was religious leaders who were concerned about the man Jesus and sought to keep him under control.

I sometimes upset people when I say we have a system of religious domination today, and it is part of the problem facing the Christian church. I am referring to any group that has turned Christianity (or any other major faith group) into a legalistic system which parallels and maybe even exceeds the legalism of the scribes and Pharisees of Jesus' time. I believe legalism is not isolated denominationally, but is almost always found in a fundamentalist approach. This "my way or go away" can range all the way from the infallibility of the Pope to the inerrancy of scripture. What is common to all legalistic systems is the proclamation of certain "correct beliefs" you must have. If you don't have them, you are in danger of going to hell, being ostracized from the religious group, excommunicated, or in the extreme, exterminated.

John Shelby Spong, a retired bishop of the Episcopal Church, USA, first introduced me to the term "believers in exile" in his book, *Why Christianity Must Change or Die*. These exiled people are believers and have experienced God, but cannot agree with what they are told they must believe. They are unwilling to accept the proclaimed "correct beliefs." They have matured religiously from the faith of their childhood and are now searching for adult religious food and are unable to find it in the religiosity of the church. They have a strong sense that there is more to Christianity than inflexible rules and rituals with which they have been saturated since childhood. They are not willing to accept "infallibility" or "inerrancy" on blind faith just because a religious institution or ecclesiastical hierarchy is telling them they must. These people are not from any one demographic group but cross the spectrums of denomination, age, race, and even socioeconomic status. Again, I want to stress I think these people still believe in their God experience, but want more than the canned answers they receive when they raise serious issues about the church or Christianity. The God box they have been handed no longer contains the answers. They don't like the decorations traditional Christianity has affixed to the God in the box. This is especially true of the decorations affixed by fundamentalist Christianity.

There is another group that has similar feelings but I see as reacting differently. This group is not sure of any real God experience and has completely thrown over being force fed and have rejected it. They are members of the "church alumni association." They are called church alumni because many of them were once active members of some organized religious group. Simplistic answers or being told to just accept something on faith turned them off. Rather than continuing the search for answers, they just tuned out and turned away. Caleb in Chapter Two would probably belong to this association. They may take with them a certain amount of bitterness and hurt. This may manifest itself

WHO IS JESUS?

in speech and behavior that shows scorn for any religious institution. In all fairness, I have to say that whatever they say caused them to leave the church is not always justified. Churches do get a lot of blame when people want to justify their action for leaving the church. There are a lot of stories out there about why people leave the church. Some stories actually depict a type of religious indignation, some are almost comical, some will depress you, and some are just downright superficial. One commonality present in most of the stories is a depiction of Christianity being forced on them. They could not buy the package, so the first chance they got they escaped. The escape mechanism was to throw over any pretense of being religious. In my opinion this is another group where the seeds are provided from which atheism sprouts.

Well, that was certainly a deviation from the process! Hopefully it will liven up the discussion somewhat. I make no apologies for including it as part of a discussion on oppressive systems. Much religion today fits the category as much as some aspects of the politics, culture, and Jewish religion at the time of Jesus fits the category.

We need to move on and look at history during the time of Jesus. One valuable source we can read is the work of Josephus. He is one of the ancient historians who provide us with information about that age. Historically, we know the homeland of Jesus was a Jewish community belonging to the Roman Empire and ruled by Roman authorities. There was always unrest among the downtrodden classes, and the Romans had to be constantly on guard for possible revolution. The small village of Jesus was probably not immune to unrest.

Jesus lived in a world that had been shaped and influenced by the reign of Herod the Great. He ruled from 37 BCE until 4 CE. Sometimes he was referred to as Herod the Monstrous. It was Rome who had selected him to rule that portion of the Roman Empire as king of the Jews. As an old saying goes, "he lived high on the hog!" He was a wild spender and spent exorbitant amounts building extravagant palaces for his own use. By birth one parent was Jewish, and so he wanted to make himself acceptable to his Jewish population. After all, an emperor accepted by those he rules is less likely to be revolted against. One of the ways he did this was by rebuilding the temple in Jerusalem. When he died, his kingdom was divided among his three sons. Galilee, where Jesus lived, went to Herod Antipas. This was the Herod of Jesus' time.

There was another change wrought by Rome in about 6 CE. The Roman Empire basically made the Jewish high priests in Jerusalem the local authorities. Between the years of 6 CE and 66 CE, eighteen high priests were appointed by Rome. You have to see this as a very calculated and smart move. The use of high priests was a strategy used to help keep the population in check and prevent uprisings. It was in this environment Jesus grew up in a small peasant village. The high priests were the mediators of Roman rule. It was their task to maintain order and to collect taxes paid to Rome. They were responsible for keeping the populace under control and preventing any sort of disobedience or uprising which might bring the wrath of Rome down upon the community. The name of the high priest we can associate with Jesus was Caiaphas. He was the high priest when the plot among the elders and chief priests was hatched leading to the arrest, trial, and crucifixion of Jesus. Jesus was a threat because he was endangering the status quo. You may have heard the saying, "Come weal or come woe my status is quo." That was the way the priests liked it. It was feared what Jesus was doing would incite some kind of rebellion. Unrest in even a small village could grow. They did see Jesus as stirring up the people. Rebellion was the last thing the priests wanted on their plate.

There is another little tidbit of information of which some people are not aware. The language of the community in which Jesus was raised was most likely Aramaic. We don't know if Jesus knew any Greek. He may have, because according to scripture he conversed with Pilot, who probably spoke Greek. They could also converse if Pilot knew Aramaic. We don't even know for sure if Jesus was literate. Aramaic would also have been the language of his disciples. This can be of significance because sometimes those who want to go back to the original words of Jesus point to scriptures written in Greek years after his death. These scriptures were not written by any of his Aramaic-speaking disciples.

WHO IS JESUS?

They were not even written by eyewitnesses. I'm sure I have upset the fundamentalists who know it was Jesus' disciples or eyewitnesses who wrote scripture, and they wrote it in the language of Jesus—Greek. That may be what they have in their God box, but it isn't in mine! In all fairness, I need to say there are some fundamentalists who do accept that the language of Jesus was Aramaic.

With that brief historical perspective, we move on to how most people get whatever knowledge they have about Jesus. Most people attempt to find out about Jesus by reading the scriptures telling about him. This is what I refer to as devotional reading, not a deep textual study. Textual study becomes a very different and difficult process if you are willing to look at the scripture critically, rather than just devotionally. How do you determine if a saying actually goes back to Jesus? It could be a story from the Old Testament, retold with Jesus as the main character. It could also be a story created by his followers. It could be a story illustrating what Jesus meant to his followers. Over a period of time, it becomes a saying coming from the mouth of Jesus. This is the type of statement that horrifies those who hold to the gospels as literal truth. Jesus was a person who taught a particular "way." Many of his early followers were Jews who still worshipped in the synagogues. Jesus himself was a Jew. In at least one place, followers of Jesus were referred to as followers of "the way" (Acts 9:2). There were also others, non-Jews, who worshipped in the synagogues. These were gentiles who were called "God fearers."

Is there a difference between the Jesus of history, the Jesus of the New Testament, and the Jesus portrayed by the Christianity of the twenty-first century? The Jesus of history was a charismatic leader who experienced God in a way not seen before or since. He was probably a mystic. We know he was a defender and helper of the poor, the weak, and the downtrodden in an oppressive society. He challenged a system that had social boundaries which discriminated against individuals in the society. These boundaries were found in both religious and political aspects. He had no boundaries in his acceptance of people regardless of gender, race, culture, or socioeconomic status. That was part of what got him in trouble. He was a man of great wisdom, and taught in hyperbole and parables to illustrate the truth he proclaimed. His teaching angered some and inspired others. He was a devout Jew, even though he challenged the Jewish leadership of his day. He even said, *"Do you think that I have come to abolish the law or the prophets; I have come not to abolish but to fulfill."* (Matthew 5:17). He was dedicated to challenging the injustices of his day. It was the way he did this and the inspiration and motivation he instilled in people that led to the beginning of the early Christian movement. Above all else, he was a man who when people looked at him saw a portrayal of God in a way God had never been seen before. Jesus completely changed what his followers had in their God boxes before they met him.

So how was Jesus portrayed by the earliest Christian writers? One of the "correct beliefs" held by fundamentalists, and many others who would not consider themselves as fundamentalists, is that Jesus was born of a virgin. This was one of the five fundamentals I listed earlier in this book. Keep in mind that the earliest New Testament writer was Paul. His letters were probably written between the years of 48 CE and his death sometime between 62-64 CE. Never once in his writings does Paul mention the virgin birth. Was it because it was such common knowledge it didn't need to be written about? Perhaps it was because it wasn't a necessary part of believing and following Jesus. The earliest gospel was Mark, believed to be written about 70 CE. This gospel relates nothing about a virgin birth. Surely if this was an important doctrine, the first gospel written should have mentioned it. The first reference to a virgin birth is found in the gospel of Matthew, then in the gospel of Luke. It is not found in the gospel of John. Why were stories of the virgin birth added to what Mark had written?

If you opened your newspaper today and the headlines told of a virgin birth, what would you think? Most reactions would have something to do with saying it was impossible. What if significant leaders in your known world had claimed virgin births? Adding to that, what if your fellow citizens believed the accounts of virgin births for some of these significant leaders, or at least went along with the stories? If the citizenry believed those in high places were offspring of a virgin birth, it might even be more readily accepted. The story you read in the newspaper might well have been to elevate the status of the person featured in the story. It is nigh on impossible for us to think that way in the twenty-first century. Now put yourself back into the first century. Wouldn't the story of the person born of a virgin elevate that person's status? This would be especially true if royalty was born in that manner.

Stories about virgin births were not unusual in the ancient world. This was an accepted method used to attach divine or at least extraordinary attributes to a king, a ruler, or significant leader. In the Roman times, the emperor was viewed as the Son of God because of divine descent. For example, Julius Caesar was a descendant of the god Venus through her son Aeneas, thus a Son of God. Caesar Augustus was considered to be divine. He had brought peace to the Roman Empire and was considered a savior because of it. Coins, inscriptions, and even temples proclaimed him as "Son of God." The Roman historians Suetonius and Dio Cassius claim that the god Apollo fathered Augustus. Were these stories believed to be factually true? Rather difficult to ask them at this point. Again, there could very well have been more of a metaphorical understanding than a literal understanding of the issue.

If these stories about Jesus' birth were so extremely important, why were they missing from the writings of Paul and of Mark? If in Roman thinking a virgin birth made one a Son of God, then would it not stand to reason applying the same concept to the conception and birth of Jesus would make Jesus a Son of God? Matthew and Luke may have been challenging the claim of Roman belief that Augustus and his successors were to be considered "Sons of God."

If we consider the stories of Matthew and Luke as factual, we are confronted with a number of differences and contradictions impossible to reconcile. I pointed out some issues surrounding genealogy earlier. It is revealing to look at some of the differences in the birth narratives. Looking at them separately rather than combined in a Christmas pageant, we can identify these differences. Matthew has the family living in Bethlehem and Jesus is born at home. The family moves to Nazareth after fleeing to Egypt. Luke tells us the family lived in Nazareth and travels to Bethlehem because of a census decree. Joseph was required to go to the town of Bethlehem, the town of David, because he was of the lineage and house of David. There are no explanations as to why Mary had to go, as only males were counted. I contend it does make for a better story. It is significant to note recorded history of that period says nothing of such a census. It would have been such a large project (if historically accurate) that surely someone else would have mentioned it. Consider another factor. If all descendants of David returned to Bethlehem to register, there would have been pandemonium. Do you have any idea how many descendents there would be since the generation of David? Definitely there would have been no room in the inn—probably no room in the whole countryside.

Our Christmas pageants mix up the story in other ways also. Matthew has wise men visit the baby Jesus, probably at home, led there by a star, but no angels announcing his birth. Luke has angels announcing his birth and shepherds visiting him in a manger. Don't get me wrong, I love the Christmas pageantry. I just believe it is unfortunate that most people see it as depicting historical events surrounding the birth of Jesus. Luke has no flight into Egypt because of the slaughter of male infants in Bethlehem. That is part of Matthew's story. The slaughter story was brought about by order of King Herod the Great based on information from the wise men. Matthew's story has the family flee to Egypt for safety. Here again is a rather significant event for which there is no recorded history of such a slaughter. I would also think if such a slaughter actually took place, it would appear in one of the other gospels. Such a drastic measure would surely have been recorded by some historian of the age. In Luke, we have two significant birth stories, Jesus and John the Baptist. Matthew lists only the birth of Jesus. In Luke, the angel's visitation is to Mary, but in Matthew it is Joseph who has an angel come to him. None of these things are insurmountable if you read the stories to find their deeper meaning. It does create a problem if you are intent on proving the stories as literal descriptions of the way things happened. If your God box includes

WHO IS JESUS?

the inerrant word of God—God dictated and man wrote—it becomes very difficult to reconcile the differences. I suppose you could say that Matthew or Luke must have had a hearing problem when God spoke to them.

The conclusion for me is the birth stories should not be read as historical. This does not mean I do not believe in the birth of Jesus. It means I do not believe the events surrounding it as recorded in Matthew and Luke are factual. The important question is not "Did it happen this way?" but "What does it mean?" Being born of a virgin in the ancient world bestowed divine or other extraordinary qualities to a king or leader. Most scholars seem to agree that the birth stories are not historical accounts of a happening. To argue that the stories are literal-factual can prevent us from discovering the true meanings contained in the stories. They are to be seen as symbolic narratives growing out of the early Christian movement and written down by Matthew and Luke. If they are symbolic, what are some of the themes the writers were trying to get across?

They both lean toward the theme of light coming into the darkness. When light appears, the darkness disappears. When Jesus came he brought new light into a world of darkness, not literally dark, but speaking of the darkness of the human condition. I believe most people are aware the birth of Jesus was not on the actual day of December 25. It was the decision of the Church in the fourth century to celebrate the birth of Jesus at the time of the winter solstice. Why did they do that? It is the darkest time of the year and expresses very well the symbolism of light coming into the darkness. It may also have been to combat some of the pagan festivals surrounding that time of the year. The symbolism of light would also have applied to bringing light to the pagans. In the Old Testament, light is seen as an image of salvation (Isaiah 9:2, 60:1-3). John certainly expounds this theme in his gospel. John depicts Jesus as the light of the world (John 1:4-9, 9:5).

Matthew and Luke were also saying Jesus was the fulfillment of the deepest hopes and dreams of ancient Israel. Jesus was to come and bring about a new kingdom on Earth. Matthew especially relies heavily

GOD IN A BOX

on Old Testament stories to show Jesus as the one who was to come. Matthew is sometimes referred to as the Jewish gospel. He seems to have a vast knowledge of Old Testament scripture. He was most probably writing to a Jewish audience and used his writing to show how Jesus fulfilled the scripture. Some twelve times he described an event as happening to fulfill the scriptures. He was without a doubt speaking about the Jewish messianic expectations and writing to fit Jesus into those expectations.

To Matthew, the birth of Jesus was a fulfillment of Isaiah 7:14, which proclaimed that a virgin would conceive and bear a son. Here I am going to get into trouble again with the fundamentalists. To translate the word in Isaiah to "virgin" is an erroneous translation. The word translated to "virgin" might better be translated as "a young woman of marriageable age." We could possibly assume a young woman of marriageable age at that time would be a virgin, but that is still reading into the translation. The New Revised Version now translates it as "...the young woman is with child..." It is entirely possible that a woman with child would not be married. Being married was not a requirement for getting pregnant then any more than it is in the present. Just as important, Isaiah was not prophesying an event to take place hundreds of years later. He was declaring a birth in the royal family should be taken as a sign Jerusalem would not fall to some foreign armies surrounding Jerusalem even as Isaiah wrote. I quote again from *The Late Liz*, "For me the truth of Christ doesn't stand or fall on whether Mary was a virgin; it stands on the change Christ made and does make in my life and in the lives of all who seek him."

It is fascinating the lengths to which some people will go to defend "correct beliefs." One of those is the belief Isaiah 7:14 can only be interpreted as "virgin." I once attended a service devoted entirely to showing the error of the Revised Standard Version in changing the King James Version word "virgin" to "young woman." For me it was a curiosity meeting as I accepted without question the change in translation. After what I considered to be much ado about nothing, it was time to support the cause. The speaker asked anyone who had currency

WHO IS JESUS?

in the amount of $20, $10, or at the very least, $5 to take the bills out and wave them in the air. Not much currency showed up. He then promised everyone that he would not ask them for their money. Bills began to show up throughout the assembly. After the bills were waving in the air, he said, "Now trade bills with your neighbor." Everyone did as directed. Then he said, "We are now going to pass the offering plates. When the offering plate comes by, put your neighbor's money in the plate. See," he said, "I'm not asking you for your money, I'm asking you for your neighbor's money." Remember earlier in the book I said the use of a "con" was deemed acceptable if truly in support of "correct beliefs"? Would this episode at least touch the edge of a "con"? You decide.

Remember the earlier explanation of how a virgin birth was used to confer "son of God" to royalty or leadership? The claim of Matthew and Luke may have been to emphasize that the virgin birth of Jesus made him the true Son of God. They wanted their followers, or any who may have heard of this new movement, to realize it was Jesus, not Caesar Augustus, who brings peace to Earth and is the true savior. You don't need the virgin birth to make a case for such a proclamation still today.

How would you describe the mission of Jesus during his earthly life? Did Jesus have a purpose? One answer you will hear is that he came as the fulfillment of Old Testament prophecy. The question then becomes one of asking what he fulfilled. An answer for many is he was the promised Messiah. For many Christians, there is an add-on: "He came to die for my sins!" But what exactly does that mean? Would it surprise you there a number of different theories about what that means? What does your God box contain concerning the mission of Jesus? You decide.

Possibly the best known and most adhered to concept is called the substitutionary theory of atonement. This name could be related to a number of different theories, all of which have Jesus dying for others. A central element of substitutionary atonement is God sent Jesus to die on the cross as a substitute for others—others including you and me. The others also include all humankind past, present, and future. An important aspect was the willingness of Jesus to go along with his own sacrificial death. This sacrificial death was willed and needed by God. As already stated, this was a sacrifice for the whole human race. After all, God is King and he wants justice! God, as payment for sin, demanded this sacrificial death. The death of Jesus and his resurrection are at the very heart of the Christian faith. Was it a sacrifice demanded by God to pay for the sins of all humankind?

Atonement is a theological word that describes an action that pays for or does away with the sins of someone else. In the Old Testament, sacrificing certain animals as a payment for one's sins brought about this atonement. An unblemished lamb is an example of an acceptable sacrifice. To whom was this payment made? Payment was made to none other than to God. God demanded it, according to the Jewish understanding of God. This was part of the Jewish God box. It was part of the legalistic system of the Jewish faith. Human beings sin, and God hates sin. Sin stands between the individual and an individual's relationship with God. God demands payment in order for the sin to be voided. The payment (atonement) must be in the form of a sacrifice.

Atonement is an arrangement by which the literal penalty deserved because of sin may be avoided by the one who committed the sin. It is something that may be substituted in the place of punishment to the sinner. In the case of all humankind, Jesus was the substitution. The death of Jesus was a sacrifice for sin. It had to happen in order to make God's forgiveness available to the rest of us. Again, please note this portrays God as primarily a lawgiver and judge (king) who demands a payment we cannot make. The payment was made by Jesus. The main problem with this is that it makes grace not free, but with requirements attached. Closely associated with this view is the belief of many that being Christian has its value and primary importance only in assuring life after death. That would seem to support why so many people say they are Christian in order to get to heaven.

Another twist to this in fundamentalist thinking is the necessity for the sacrifice to be a blood sacrifice. In Jewish practice the lamb, or

WHO IS JESUS?

other sacrificial animal, was killed in a specified liturgical procedure. The blood was then smeared on the mercy seat of God in the Holy of Holies in the Jewish Temple. It was believed through some divine or magical power, the blood had a cleansing effect, doing away with or at least covering over the sins of the people. A favorite Bible verse often quoted here is Hebrews 9:22, *"...without the shedding of blood there is no forgiveness of sins."* This is another one of those items falling under "correct beliefs." If you don't believe in the blood theory, you certainly can't be a Christian. If Jesus had been hanged, drowned, suffocated, or killed in some other manner, without blood being shed, his death would have been to no avail. All this is reading back into Old Testament scripture and ancient Jewish beliefs. That could lead to a whole new discussion, and I don't intend to go there. Also note that I started the quote from Hebrews after three little dots, known as an ellipsis. It means I omitted a part of the verse preceding what I quoted. What I left out—and it is generally left out by the "shed blood" advocates—is *"Indeed, under the law almost everything is purified by blood..."* "Almost everything" is a qualifier that leaves a lot to conjecture. What is included and what is not? Ask a fundamentalist, and you will get the answer. That doesn't mean it is correct, but to the fundamentalist it helps keep their theory intact.

Why couldn't God just forgive sins without the need of a sacrifice? That is indeed possible. I believe God could, but the God in the God box of many people could not. That destroys many Christians' concept of God. Remember the monarchal concept? God as king is believed to require compensation because he is both lawgiver and judge, and disobedience requires punishment or compensation. The sacrifice of Jesus is the compensation that was required. Like a king who loves his subjects, God's love was so great he provided the sacrifice. The sacrifice God provided was Jesus.

Think about it for a moment. If you are a parent, you know firsthand children sometimes disobey and deserve punishment. As a parent, you have the power and the authority to mete out due punishment as deserving of the disobedience. How many times did you just forgive

GOD IN A BOX

and forget because you also had the power of forgiveness? Does disobedience have to be followed by punishment to meet the requirements of justice? No, it does not, yet the fundamentalist mindset perceives of a God who is not as forgiving as a loving parent. To say that God requires compensation or retribution—based on the Old Testament concept of sacrifice for forgiveness—describes a God who is unforgiving unless there is due payment. It makes Jesus a victim of that unforgiving being. That is not the picture of God I hold in my God box. I say again, God is love, and love is of God. How could a loving God do an unloving act? What would be the unloving act? Demanding the death of Jesus to meet the required payment would not be a loving act!

If we are truly sinners, where did sin originate? In the fundamentalist mind, it has been part of our nature since "the fall." I'm talking about the Garden of Eden, the forbidden fruit, and Adam and Eve being kicked out by God. The story goes that their disobedience brought sin into the world, which has been the lot of humankind ever since. But what if the story of the Garden of Eden is not historical? How do we inherit the sin of a myth? I don't believe the story is historical, so for me there is no historical "fall" by humankind. Besides, doesn't the Genesis story tell us God looked at all creation and proclaimed it was good? If all creation was good, then was the snake that tempted Eve also good? Was the snake not a part of all creation? What transpired to make it not good? What happened to make man evil? The easy answer is because Adam and Eve ate the forbidden fruit and were cast out of the Garden of Eden. That answer is based on accepting the Garden of Eden myth as historical and literal. As I don't see it as literal and historical, that answer is unacceptable. For me, there was no first man and first woman created directly by God. There was no snake! I realize I am raising as many questions as I am answering. This does not bother me, as I believe it is in asking the questions that we grow and develop our faith. I certainly do not have a set of "correct beliefs" in my God box. I do have a set of beliefs that are not set in concrete and continue to expand, raise new questions, provide new insights, and yes, sometimes even change. They are my "God in a box" beliefs, but I keep the lid off

WHO IS JESUS?

the box. I don't believe I can contain God in a box.

I have certainly gone a long way around to get at the mission of Jesus and still haven't given an answer. I did believe it was important to deal with some things I thought were not the answers. Books have been written exploring his mission much better than I can, but I still need to put in my two cents' worth. After all the detours you may be expecting something of great insight and astounding truth. That will not be the case.

There is one thing of which we can be sure. Jesus defied the religious authorities and oppressive powers of his day. Why else were those who were holders of religious power out to do away with him? He was living the kingdom of God as he believed it should be lived on Earth and invited others to live it with him. The way he lived upset the leaders of the Jewish legalistic system. He upset the system by saying religious rules are not moral or justified unless they enhance the lives of humankind. I like to think he was attempting to show that in spite of thousands of years of human experience, and the role of religion in human experience, the primary purpose of religion is not to please some supernatural deity, but to improve quality of life for all humankind. Maybe that is something we need to look at again in the twenty-first century!

I mentioned earlier that Jesus faced an oppressive society and he was a defender of those considered to be the underdogs of society. The Jewish people were an oppressed society. Unless you were a member of the ruling class, you were oppressed, whether you were Jewish or gentile. What do oppressed people do? They find ways to resist. Certainly we have many stories of Jewish revolts and overt resistance. Revolts and overt resistance would be a very active violent resistance. There is also nonviolent resistance. It can be active resistance even though non-violent. To illustrate from more recent history, the resistance of a Mahatma Gandhi or a Martin Luther King would be nonviolent resistance. I like to think of Jesus as a Jewish revolutionary who pursued justice through nonviolent but active resistance.

A couple of examples may help illustrate. First, why did Jesus ride a donkey into Jerusalem? Conquerors rode a horse on their victory entrance into a city. Jesus chose a donkey, possibly to illustrate the contrast between the kingdom he was proclaiming and the type of kingdom portrayed by a conqueror. He was proclaiming that the message of the Kingdom of God was a kingdom of peace, not of war, not of vanquishing people, and not of violence. A little sidelight here for the fundamentalists who might be brave enough still to be reading this. If you read the accounts as literal and inerrant, there is a problem with the account of the triumphal entry in Matthew 21. It has Jesus riding into Jerusalem on both a donkey and her colt. Don't believe me? Matthew 21:7 reads, "...*they brought the donkey and the colt, placed their cloaks on them and he sat upon them."* Now how did he do that?

The cleansing of the temple is another example of Jesus resisting the way things were done. Why did he cleanse the temple? Why did he call it a *"...den of robbers"* (Luke 19:45)? Jesus must have known it was necessary to have money changers to convert currency so worshippers could pay their taxes and purchase animals for sacrifice. His anger may have been directed at the Jewish authority figures. Their collaboration with Roman authorities created a system in which the people ended up being cheated—even when carrying out religious requirements.

I need to throw in a little zinger here for the enlightenment of the *inerrancy of scripture* crowd. This falls into the area of their claim that there are no discrepancies or contradictions in scripture. In Matthew the cleansing of the temple takes place at the end of Jesus' ministry, Matthew 21:12-13. In John it takes place at the beginning of Jesus' ministry, John 2:12-14. How do you reconcile this difference? If you are more interested in "What does it mean?" than "Did it really happen this way?" you don't have a problem. For the inerrancy group, this is the type of issue where they play ostrich—they hide their heads in the sand and hope it will go away. Some will answer that you just have to have faith. Faith in what I don't know, and I'm not sure they do.

Jesus definitely had a vision of how life on Earth should be lived if God was running the show instead of the Jewish hierarchy and Roman authorities. Jesus sincerely believed he was ushering in the Kingdom

WHO IS JESUS?

of God on Earth. He often referred to the "Son of Man." He was not referring to himself when he did. When the "Son of Man" came, things would be different. The kingdom envisioned by Jesus was much different than the oppressive system in control during his time. He was upsetting the Jewish authorities by offering forgiveness to all without the necessity of going through "correct liturgical rituals." The "correct" in reference to liturgical rituals prescribed by the Jewish hierarchy in the time of Jesus is only different in content from the "correct" in reference to beliefs the fundamentalist says you must have in our time. Both are examples of oppressive controlling religious systems contrary to the teachings of Jesus. Bishop John Shelby Spong, in his book *Jesus for the Non-Religious*, states, "Moralism and righteousness finally never issue in love or new life; they issue only in law and religious control. The quest for humanity is not the same as the quest to be religious."

The mission of Jesus was to show the great compassion God had for all people. Jesus may have been the first to recognize the importance of the individual. For Jesus, there was not Gentile, Jew, Samaritan, male, female, or whatever other category you want to list. For Jesus all were people for whom God had compassion. Jesus was a revelation to humankind. Through his death Jesus revealed what God is like—not an ogre demanding payment for sin. Rather, the presence of God, the ground of all being, is a presence filled with compassion and love for all humankind. It is a presence that directs us to do the same. The life of Jesus points to life as a process of spiritual transformation. The life of Jesus is an example of giving all that he was to whoever came into contact with him, thus revealing what God is like. Paul may have said it best in Romans 8:38-39, *"For I am convinced that neither death, nor life, nor angels, nor rulers, nor things present, nor things to come, nor powers, nor height, nor depth, nor anything else in all creation, will be able to separate us from the love of God in Christ Jesus our Lord."* Jesus gave all, including his life at its prime, not as sacrifice for sin, but to show just how great this love from God is. Understanding this is the greatest thing you could have in your God box. What more do you want or need? I know—some of you need "correct beliefs"!

GOD IN A BOX

Jesus was executed in one of the cruelest methods of his time. Why did this happen and who did it? Simply stated, Jesus was executed because he was a threat to the established oppressive order. I would include in the established order both the Roman Empire and the Jewish hierarchy. There is no one group that bears the blame. There is little doubt about whether there was collusion among the ruling elites of the time—both religious and political. At the least it would certainly involve Pilate and the Jewish temple authorities.

The Jewish people were an oppressed people, and the Jewish temple authorities were party to that oppression. I will be so bold as to say the Jewish temple authorities were more interested in obedience to the law than compassion for the people. They didn't want anyone in the Jewish community rocking the boat. Jesus was a threat in two ways. First, he challenged the authority of the Jewish religious hierarchy. Second, he was seen as a threat to the religious status quo, even if not a real threat to peace with the Roman rulers. Trouble in the Jewish community could bring down wrath from the Roman authorities. Things were going smoothly until the troublemaker Jesus appeared on the scene. Jesus challenged the system, and that challenge cost him his life.

The crucifixion is one thing in scripture that can be accepted as historically certain. That does not mean all accounts surrounding it in the New Testament are historically accurate. Some of those accounts are undoubtedly remembered actual events. There probably was a last supper. There probably was an arrest leading up to the crucifixion. There was a crucifixion. There is little doubt about the historicity of these events. Some events had to have been filled in by the imagination of his followers. An example would be the events of the trial. The scripture tells us all of his followers fled after his arrest. If true, who were the eyewitnesses providing an account of the events? I doubt if there was a scribe there taking notes. How do we know the words Jesus prayed in the Garden of Gethsemane? Jesus had gone some distance from the disciples, and they had fallen asleep. Did Jesus have a written copy of his prayer which he gave the disciples before or after he prayed? I am certain he did not have a small handheld digital recorder on which his words were saved for posterity.

Some events were written to prove the fulfillment of Old Testament prophecy. Psalm 22 and Isaiah 53 would be examples. The death of Jesus was necessary, foretold, destined to happen, and happened just the way it was foretold. This means some details of the last week were not events someone present for the events remembered. They were prophecies from the Old Testament turned into history by the gospel writers. Being more specific, Mark 15:24 probably came from Psalm 22:18. Matthew 27:34 came from Psalm 69:21. Mark 15:33, referring to darkness from noon to 3:00 PM is symbolic, rather than historical. That thought most likely came from a combination of sources, Exodus 10:21-23, Jeremiah 15:9, and Amos 8:9.

A question that needs to be asked is, "Was the death of Jesus the will of God?" To my way of thinking, the answer is an emphatic NO! I know that contradicts the fundamentalist idea that God needed a sacrifice and Jesus was the designated victim. I don't think it is ever the will of God for someone to be executed. I don't believe it was the will of God when the Israelites slaughtered their enemies because they believed God told them to do so. That is different from saying the Israelites did not believe God told them to do the slaughter. Another question to ask is, "Was the death of Jesus inevitable?" That is entering different territory. I believe it was inevitable not because God willed it, but because execution was the lot of those who bucked the system. Jesus bucked the system. What better way to discourage any other wannabes?

The story does not end with the crucifixion. Next is what we now celebrate on Easter Sunday, the resurrection. It is without doubt the event most central and significant to the Christian faith. It is questionable if we would ever have heard about Jesus if not for this event. But do we know what really happened? Without the resurrection, there would be no Christian church. Was this the greatest miracle of the centuries? Is this the doorway to a promise of life after death? We are again looking at an issue that if not literally true would destroy the faith of many believers. It would have the greatest impact on those of fundamentalist beliefs, but certainly not limited to them. Does it have to be a literal event to have significant meaning to Christians of all generations in the past, present, and future? I don't think so.

The New Testament gives a timeline for the death and resurrection of Jesus. Is this to be considered a literal, historical sequence of events? If it is, we need to clear up some confusion among the gospel writers. There are some differences in their timelines. The days and timelines may have had more symbolic significance than literal happenings. What is not often considered is the possibility the events described may have taken place over a period of time—as long as months. The followers of Jesus were puzzled by his death and wanted to make sense out of what happened. They couldn't explain the events, but they continued to feel his presence with them and felt empowered by him. They believed he continued to be a part of their lives. Those who believed in him before he was crucified continued to believe in him after his crucifixion. Two historians of ancient times, Tacitus, a Roman, and Josephus, a Jew, speak about Jesus. They do not relate a story of resurrection but do talk about a movement in which followers continued to follow Jesus. It was difficult for the followers of Jesus to accept Jesus was dead. Why was this? Is it possible it was because in some strange way they kept experiencing his presence with them as something very real? Is it possible the presence they felt was so real they believed Jesus was right there with them as they continued the mission he had started?

The question asked of me at this point is, "Do you believe in the resurrection?" My answer will depend on what you mean by resurrection. If you mean do I believe in a physically resuscitated body, my answer is no. There are other stories in the Bible that tell about people being raised from the dead. I don't believe any of them ever literally happened. Next, I will be accused of not believing in the resurrection. Wrong! I may not believe in your version of the resurrection. But that something very real happened to the followers of Jesus after his crucifixion I have absolutely no doubts.

I listened to what I would call a Christian mystic speak in a church service. I don't remember the name, but do remember the thrust of her message. She talked about her walk with Jesus. This was something she

WHO IS JESUS?

claimed happened more than once. Jesus would appear to her and she would carry on a conversation with him. She even related some of the conversations; Jesus said…I said… Could this be proven in any way but by her sharing it happened to her? I doubt it. Could she have been experiencing the same type of presence felt by the disciples after the death of Jesus? That is entirely within the realm of possibility. From time to time, we hear stories about someone who has a vision of Jesus. It would be wrong to discount those stories. You may not believe the stories, but there is no way you can prove they didn't happen. The visions are very real to those who experience them. I believe the presence of Jesus to those who saw him after his death was no less real. I also believe those sightings were not of a resuscitated physical body.

Without the resurrection there would be no Christianity! How else would you describe his followers' intense sense that he was still with them? We have here the same difficulty we have when we attempt to describe God. When language fails us, we still have to use words in an attempt to describe what is indescribable. Is it possible that resurrection is the word that best described what the followers of Jesus continued to feel about his presence? I said they felt as empowered by his presence after his death as they had before. Doesn't that imply in some way Jesus was still with them? How could this possibly be true? If not true in a literal, physical sense, they must have experienced him in some other way. This may be one of those things we cannot answer but only accept. What does seem clear is they experienced the presence of Jesus with them in spite of his death—that is the Easter story. That should still be the Easter story in the life of any person who claims to be a Christian. Not how did it happen, but has it happened in the life of the individual? Paul said it very well. *"…if Christ has not been raised, then our proclamation has been in vain and your faith has been in vain."* (I Corinthians 15:14). Was Paul talking about a resuscitated physical body or was he trying to describe a presence experienced in a manner that had never before happened? He doesn't say. That means you have to decide. I choose a new presence in a new way. Remember, Paul also says later in that same chapter that flesh and blood cannot inherit the

GOD IN A BOX

kingdom (I Corinthians 15:50). To my way of thinking, that would also include a resuscitated Jesus. You decide.

One final note needs to be given about the resurrection and presence. Believe it or not, I believe the answer to how Jesus continues to live is contained in a hymn used regularly at Easter. The hymn "He Lives" is used across the theological spectrum from liberals to fundamentalists. The first stanza reads in part, "I serve a risen Savior, he's in the world today; I know that he is living, whatever foes may say." Then the last line of the refrain speaks to what I personally believe. It also describes what I believe took place on that first Easter: "You ask me how I know he lives? He lives within my heart." Those words were the answer to the resurrection story of Jesus in the first century. Those words are still the answer to the resurrection story of Jesus in the twenty-first century. What a powerful statement! Do we need any more than those words? Those words would be an important addition to anyone's God box. You decide.

This chapter would not be complete without a few words about the Second Coming of Jesus. I cannot leave it out, as it is such an integral part of fundamentalist belief. But what does it all mean? It must mean a lot of different things, because there are hundreds, if not thousands, of books that have been written to explain it. I will readily admit this has been an expectation of the Christian tradition since its inception in the first century. It is generally associated with what is often called "the end of the ages," or "the end of time," or "the last days." To put it into a theological term, it is often referred to as apocalyptic eschatology. Do not get hung up on that phrase. Just think of it in terms of end times.

There is little doubt Paul expected it to happen within a short time. His epistle to the church at Thessalonica (1 Thessalonians) certainly promoted this theme. Even Jesus appears to be apocalyptic in his thinking. In Mark 9:1 he says, *"Truly I say to you, there are some standing here who will not taste death until they see that the Kingdom of God has come with power."* In Matthew 10:23 he says, *"When they persecute you in one town, flee to the next; for truly I tell you, you will not have gone through all the towns of Israel before the Son of Man comes."* I don't know how

WHO IS JESUS?

the fundamentalists deal with this. Either Jesus didn't know what he was talking about or we have misunderstood the message. I believe that Jesus absolutely believed the end was near and was simply mistaken. If true, horror of horrors, Jesus wasn't perfect. The author of Revelation certainly seemed to expect it. I do not plan to go there. Revelation is another world.

It is important to know end-time thinking (apocalyptic eschatology) was very strong during the time of Jesus. Within the Jewish faith, resurrection was seen as an "end time" event. Attach to that the belief Jesus had been resurrected and believed to be *"...the first fruits of those who died"* (1 Corinthians 15:20). It would seem logical to progress to the next step and believe an end-time general resurrection would soon follow. The destruction of the Temple may also have added credibility to the "end time is near" belief. Attach this to the conviction Jesus was Lord (made so by the virgin birth—discussed earlier in this chapter) and you have everything you need to proclaim the Jesus who had been executed by the powers of the world would soon return to judge that world.

I believe Jesus and Paul, as well as first century Christians, were "end time is near" believers. I believe they were obviously wrong—we are still here! I believe the book of Revelation was written in a code understood by early Christians. The early Christians would have understood the symbolic imagery. I also believe it refers to the Roman Empire in the first century and should not be translated to refer to some future "end time" scenario. If you can keep from getting caught up in all the imagery, Revelation in its simplest interpretation makes the case that Jesus is Lord and Rome is not!

The second coming as popularly portrayed (Jesus descending on a cloud or whatever) is not part of my belief system. Where would this return take place to enable the whole world to see it? My belief system does not preclude the reality of a second coming. I just don't see it as Jesus riding in on the clouds. I would be more in tune with the second coming happening when a person realizes the reality of Jesus and sees him as one who can transform one's life. I am speaking of a transformation brought on by following and doing what Jesus taught, not by holding "correct beliefs." Tying this to an earlier thought, maybe this is the meaning of the resurrection for that person.

Judgment is also considered a part of the end-time scenario. I believe the New Testament makes a case that what we do while we live does matter. A fundamentalist friend (yes, I do have some) told me the hereafter is important because what you do "here" will determine where you are "after." Implied in that was the idea that I would either go to heaven or hell depending on whether I held the "correct beliefs." He probably believed where I went would depend on what happens when I stand before "the great white throne" (Revelation 20:11-13) and am judged. This is sometimes referred to as the judgment bar of God. A judgment bar of God is not something you will find in my God box. I am impressed by the words of Jesus in Matthew 25:31-46. You might want to look up this story of the sheep and the goats. Please note that the criterion by which judgment is made is not what you believe but what you do. The point seems boldly clear: If you acted in compassion you are in, and if you did not act in compassion, you are out.

Finally, is Jesus the only way to God? If you are a fundamentalist, there is only one correct answer—YES! I would wager to say if you asked a fundamentalist if God and Jesus were Christians, the answer would again be—YES! How easily we turn our own biases into absolute truth. Remember that when we create our gods, they tend to look and act like we do? So it is when looking at pathways to God. Do you want to know what is in my God box? Let me give my answer right up front. No, I don't believe Jesus is the only way to God! For my belief system, I will say through Jesus is the best way for me to see and experience God.

When Bailey Smith was president of the Southern Baptist Convention (1980), he made the following statement: "God Almighty does not hear the prayer of a Jew. For how in the world can God hear the prayer of a man who says that Jesus Christ is not the true Messiah?" What does that mean? I can't answer that because he didn't say. I can disagree with it and I do! Franklin Graham has made a statement to the

WHO IS JESUS?

effect the Muslim God and the Christian God are different. How many different gods are there? There are probably as many different gods as human beings perceive there to be. But isn't there just one ground of being God?

There are many Christians—not just fundamentalists—who are convinced belief in Jesus (think "correct beliefs") is the only way to be saved. What does being saved mean? I am convinced for most Christians being saved means going to heaven when you die. Remember the majority who say their main reason for being a Christian is to get to heaven? The main proof-text for this view is John 14:6, *"I am the way, and the truth, and the life. No one comes to the Father except through me."* The fundamentalists love this verse. The televangelists proclaim it boldly from the TV pulpits. Missionaries cite it as the main impetus for going to the heathen.

John 14:6 is one of a list of "I am" saying the author of the gospel of John attributes to Jesus. Modern scholarship, among them the Jesus Seminar, states Jesus probably never said any of these things. There, I have done it again. I have offended those who take the scriptures as literal and inerrant. How can I do that? It's easy; I'm willing to use rational thought to evaluate findings of reliable Christian scholars. Again, reliable critical Christian scholarship is critical scholarship that studies scripture without preconceived ideas about what the outcome should be.

We need to look at the situation of Jewish Christians when the gospel of John was written. All was not good for the Christian community. The early Jewish Christians who had been worshipping in the synagogues had been kicked out. They were accused of no longer being a part of the faith of their fathers. Possibly one of the reasons they were kicked out was the early Christian belief that you did not have to be circumcised and become a Jew before becoming a Christian. That idea was unacceptable to Jewish leaders of the synagogue. I'm sure it was much more complicated than this, but you get the picture. They were going in different directions. John may have been written in part as a response to this action of being forcibly removed from synagogue

GOD IN A BOX

worship. The Christians banned from the temple began to say the God who revealed himself to Moses in the burning bush as the "I am" (Exodus 3:14) was the same God revealed in Jesus. The Jesus "I am" sayings recorded in John may have been used to prove Jesus was the new Moses. It was also to counter the charge those who called themselves Christians were no longer following the faith of their fathers. There was much animosity between those deposed Jewish Christians and synagogue Jews. Much of John was written to counter attacks from the Jewish community and to show why Jesus was the more excellent and only way to God.

How closely have you read the gospels? Tell me where in the gospels Jesus lists the requirements for salvation. This is not to discount the "I am" sayings in John. John is the least historical of all the gospels and was certainly written more metaphorically than literally. To see Jesus is certainly to see God. To see Jesus is to see love in action. We have already stated that "God is love." Could it be that coming to the Father (love) through Jesus (love) means it is only if we love as Jesus loved (and we can never measure up to Jesus) we can truly experience God? It makes sense to me. Jesus was compassionate and he gave us a picture of the compassion of God. Again, I say we experience God through showing the same kind of compassion shown by Jesus. Showing compassion is a process, not a finished product!

There is another interesting verse, John 6:44: *"No one can come to me unless drawn by the Father who sent me;"* You don't hear as much about this verse. What do we have here, a foreboding of predestination? Does this imply that God draws some to Jesus and others he does not? If not, why not? Surely this God of love would not leave anyone out. I have heard it said you can find something in the Bible to prove almost anything. I don't hold to that view, but some do. You can point out verses in the Bible pointing to universalism, exclusivism, and inclusivism.

There is not just one approach to what is deemed necessary for "salvation" and determination of who will be "saved." In Matthew 25, Jesus seems to indicate that actions are what are important. Paul in

WHO IS JESUS?

Ephesians 2:8-9 stresses the importance of faith. In the short book of James we are told faith without actions is of no avail (James 2:14-17). What is true for most people, whatever approach is held, my words won't change them. How is it so many Christians who believe Jesus taught compassion, inclusive love, and forgiveness believe unless a person has the "correct beliefs" about Jesus they will be damned to hell for eternity—or at least separated from God for eternity? Does it boil down to "correct beliefs" or doing what Jesus did—showing compassion? I refer you again to the story of the sheep and the goats in Matthew 25.

For me to say I see God through the example of Christ, which is the view I hold, is different from saying that everyone else has to experience God the same way. I have met some very godly people (translate as love in action—remember God is love) who were not Christian. I would not want to belittle their faith in any way, and I often learned from them. It is impossible to convince most fundamentalist Christians that someone like that could be godly. They refuse to believe there are good Muslims, Hindus, Jews, or those who practice other major faiths who can have a close relationship with God. To even go close to that concept is a major threat to Christian fundamentalist faith. This might be a good place to bring up words of Jesus from John 10:16, *"I have other sheep that do not belong to this fold. I must bring them also; and they will listen to my voice. So there will be one flock, one shepherd."* Now what do you do with that one? What does it mean? Who are the other sheep? I know there can be many explanations. I also believe the explanation will depend on your mindset. Whatever is said becomes an interpretation, not necessarily to be equated with fact.

The Jesus of the gospels was an amazing person who revealed the inclusion and compassion of God. I believe Jesus can change the lives of those who allow themselves to be transformed by his example and teaching. It could even be called a "conversion experience," a conversion that goes beyond simply holding up your hand or walking down an aisle and saying, "I believe." The belief has to be lived, not just spoken. Unless it is lived, it is not really proclaimed! Jesus can change how

GOD IN A BOX

we see God and how we should live. This does not mean God cannot be seen as compassionate and inclusive of other faiths. I like the words of Peter as recorded in Acts 10:34-35, *"Then Peter began to speak to them: 'I truly understand that God shows no partiality, but in every nation anyone who fears him and does what is right is acceptable to him."* Important words are *"does what is right."* Note it does not say "believe what is right." True Christianity is more "doing" than "believing"! If you are actively involved in the doing, the believing will take care of itself. I recall a narrative about the blind men of Cathay who were taken to see an elephant. Each took hold of the elephant in a different place and had a different view of how the elephant looked. Of course the trunk felt different than the ear. Of course a tusk felt different than a leg. All their views were different, but they were describing the same elephant. So it is as we try to describe God from our perspective.

So what does it mean to be a Christian? To believe in Jesus is not simply to believe Jesus was, but to do what Jesus did. I know I fail in that miserably, but it does not mean I should quit trying. Jesus shows me the importance and power of love, forgiveness, and compassion. The Christian life is about being aware of the God presence in everything I do. It is about my relationships with other people. Jesus shows me how to do that. This is not a journey in which I work hard to make sure I have the "correct beliefs." It is a journey in which I seek how I can be as compassionate even as Jesus showed compassion during his life on Earth. This same Jesus somehow after his death continued to live in and through those who followed him. Just as important, he still lives through his followers to this day. This is the motivation for a journey that is never complete but involves continuing transformation! I quote again the words from Micah 6:8, *"He has told you, O mortal, what is good; and what does the Lord require of you but to do justice, and to love kindness, and to walk humbly with your God?"*

Jesus loved without reservation, he gave without hesitation, and he lived without trepidation. That is the challenge standing in front of Christians of any generation and any Christian faith group. Who is Jesus to you? You decide.

5

MIRACLES: WHAT, WHY, AND HOW?

Looking at miracles is important because I believe everyone has some opinion about miracles in their God box. There is much that happens in our world that is unexplainable. How else would you explain the interest people have in the paranormal, that which lies in the twilight zone, and that which seems to be one step beyond? There have been many books written along these lines as well as many books written on healing miracles. Can we honestly say there is nothing to them? I don't think so. Can we say all things put in print can be validated? Again, I don't think so.

The subject of miracles has fascinated me for many years, particularly healing miracles. Years ago I even attended an Oral Roberts healing service. I didn't see any miracles performed, but did hear it proclaimed that miracles were taking place. I also noted those coming to be healed were screened, and only certain ones were allowed onto the stage. My seminary thesis (of which I can no longer find a copy) was on "The Healing Ministry of Jesus as Found in the Gospel of Luke." As you all know, healings are often referred to as miracles.

What could be classified as a miracle? It is sometimes defined as an extremely rare event that may or may not be scientifically or medically validated. An example of a true miracle to me would be the re-growing of a limb or a body organ. To my knowledge, it has never been achieved, at least in human beings. Yes, I know the liver has the ability to regenerate when partially removed. How about an arm or a leg? Does that mean it will never happen? Much research has been done to discover how to do that very thing. We also know regeneration of body parts does happen to some members of the animal world. If humans ever achieve that ability, will it be a miracle or a discovery of heretofore unknown information? Another area often covered by miracles is an event that defies the laws of nature. Maybe it would be better defined as an event that *seemingly* defies the known laws of nature. Do we have absolute proof we know all the laws of nature? An airplane crashes and all the people escape unharmed. It is referred to as a miracle—but was it? Maybe it was due to the expertise of the crew. If a person stepped off the roof of a tall building and, rather than plummeting, floated to the ground, I might have to reconsider my stand on miracles.

For many people, a miracle is any event in which what happened was contrary to what would ordinarily be expected to happen. Here is where we may see a big difference. I would refer to such an event as an unexplainable event. I would describe an unexplainable event as something that happens for which we have no adequate explanation—at least based on the known facts. Another explanation might be to call it a marvel—not a miracle.

Let us look now at what could be considered a religious definition of a miracle. It is often defined as a supernatural deity intervening in the known laws of nature and making something happen that without deity intervention would not have happened. It is an act of God intruding into the laws of nature. It is an unbelievable act by a supernatural deity. To me, it is important to remember a recorded miracle is not necessarily something provable; rather it is a statement about the impression the event made on those who observed it. I read a quote somewhere from Aristotle in which he said, "It is not the facts which divide men but the interpretation of the facts." That is certainly true of miracles.

MIRACLES: WHAT, WHY, AND HOW?

Looking at miracles in the Bible we have to remember the age in history and the scientific knowledge available in that age. Stories were used by the Hebrew people to transmit timeless truths from one generation to another. It is the spiritual truths transmitted by these stories that are most important, not the recorded happenings around the event. For example, there are still those in our world who believe the creation story in Genesis is an actual, recorded historical event. Let me say right now, it is not a story about how the world began. By any definition, if truly literal and historical, it would qualify as a miracle. However, the true purpose of the creation story is not to inform us about the how of creation, but to point to the power behind creation. This makes it plausible and acceptable for the ground of being to be the power behind the process of evolution. The power behind it is God, who I recognize as the source of all existence. I refer again to Paul Tillich and his discussion in *Systematic Theology Vol. I*, where he talks about God as the ground of being. To state it differently, God is the ground upon which all being is based and from which all being springs forth. God is not a being but the ground of being. The chapter on God gave a more lengthy explanation.

Miracle stories and stories of exceptional happenings were very much a part of biblical time's culture. It was no doubt a way in which they conveyed to others of different beliefs the supernatural nature and power of the God they followed and in whom they placed their trust. Of utmost importance is to keep in mind their world was not the world as we now know it. In their world, it was sin that caused sickness. In their world, mental illness and epilepsy were caused by demon possession. In their world, they lived in a three-storied universe. Viewed through that filter, everything would look very different than it does today.

Do miracles actually occur? The answer to that question will depend on who you ask. For much of the history of Christendom the answer has been a resounding YES! The Bible says so and it is the infallible word of God, so of course miracles happened. That is still the position held by fundamentalists in the twenty-first century—and held by many who would not consider themselves to be fundamentalists. If you are a fundamentalist and the Bible says it happened, it must be true. Is belief in miracles a result of humankind's need to believe there is a supernatural deity out there somewhere who if needed will intervene on their behalf if a dire need arises? Evangelists who claim to have healing powers do attract their share of followers, so there must be a sizeable population who believes it is true—or at least hopes it is.

Miracle stories are certainly in evidence throughout the Bible, beginning with the book of Genesis. Remember, those who wrote the Bible believed in a three-tiered universe. God resided in or above the sky tier and was responsible for all that happened on Earth. If that was your belief, you would certainly believe God could reach down and intervene whenever necessary—especially if the person or persons had enough faith. Ever see an athlete point to the sky or kneel after some fantastic play or score? It happens in every sport. Tim Tebow of the Denver Broncos football team was the poster boy for this during the 2011 professional football season. This behavior encourages an image of God as a kind of supernatural Santa Claus who is keeping records of "who is naughty and who is nice," and rewarding accordingly. Certainly throughout the Bible the natural laws of the universe were assumed to be in God's control. An external supernatural deity becomes extremely important for belief in miracles.

Where did this originate? Most likely it originated when humankind became self-conscious, and with that came the realization that being born was terminal. All animal life will die, and it is a cold, cruel world. It is only the human animal who has conscious knowledge of this inevitable end! With this new realization came a need to seek whatever could protect the human animal from the "terminal" happening too soon. That brought to the forefront the belief that somewhere in the sky was a supernatural deity who could watch over us. I say "could" watch over us because whether he "would" might depend on whether we were pleasing the supernatural deity. The issue then becomes figuring out what the supernatural deity desires. Once we figure that out, it becomes a behavior-controlling mechanism. This is a major factor in

MIRACLES: WHAT, WHY, AND HOW?

fundamentalists' "correct beliefs." What is not recognized is how this becomes an avenue in the manipulation of God for our own good. In our efforts to not become terminal too soon, we might need a miracle some day. We probably can't get a miracle from an angry God! What do angry people do? Multiply that by infinite anger and you have a God you don't want to irritate. You guessed it, we are back at the necessity for "correct beliefs."

The Bible tells us what this supernatural angry God can do. He actually is capable of commanding and condoning acts that most of us would consider immoral. He caused the great flood that destroyed the Earth. All ages were killed, with no mercy for women or children. When Moses was working to get the Israelites out of Egypt, God made the decision that the firstborn in every Egyptian household would die. Not to be forgotten is scripture telling us God hardened the heart of Pharaoh. Now why would God do that unless he took some kind of pleasure in bringing the plagues down upon the Egyptians? Do not forget this supernatural God kept the sun in the sky to provide more daylight to enable Joshua to see and kill more Amorites. A gory example are the she-bears Elisha brought out of the woods to ravage forty-two boys who had cursed him (2 Kings 2:23-25). Don't forget who gave him the power to do this. God must have been insulted as well. What we need to understand is, biblically speaking, a belief in miracles and a supernatural God who performed them was a major part of understanding God in biblical times.

Two of the main personalities in the Old Testament thought to speak for God were Moses and Elijah. Most Christians are familiar with Moses as the one who led the Israelites from bondage in Egypt. Not as well known is Elijah, who some consider to be the father of the prophetic movement in Judaism. I mention these two men because they were considered miracle workers in the Bible. Both of these men divided bodies of water, allowing people to walk on dry land (Exodus 14:21-22, Joshua 3:12-16). Both were believed able to manipulate nature (1 Kings 17:1ff, 2 Kings 6:1ff). Both were able to provide a supply of food (1 Kings 17:8ff, 2 Kings 4:1-8). They also had the power to raise the dead (1 Kings 17:17ff, 2 Kings 4:18-37). Remember I said in Chapter III, Who is Jesus, that biblical stories were recycled and told about Jesus to make him the new Moses and new Elijah? Do any of the above miracles sound like miracles of Jesus? How about feeding the multitudes? What about raising Lazarus from the dead?

What is obvious are the miracles of both Moses and Elijah were always in support of what was best for the Jewish people. If you look at miracles performed by lesser personalities, it also stands they were for what was best for the Jewish people, and the miracles performed often could not be proclaimed as morally justifiable. I mentioned some examples earlier, and the question still remains, why were miracles necessary? If we read scripture literally, without miracles it is doubtful the Jewish people would have survived. If they were the chosen people, then it was important to show how God looked out for them. It also sends a subtle message that God will do what is necessary to save and protect those who worship and follow him—by causing miracles if necessary. Is this a true message? Does God protect all who follow him—with miracles if necessary? What's in your God box concerning this? You decide.

In any study of miracles and the supernatural, the subject of theodicy may arise. Theodicy is basically the attempt to reconcile God's love with the presence of so much evil in the world. If God is a supernatural deity who intervenes in history, why do we see his interventions on some occasions and not on others? To put it another way, if God is all-powerful and all-loving, why is there evil in the world?

I spent a year in Vietnam as a chaplain. One of my duties during the last seven months was to provide chaplain ministries to a First Infantry Division dust-off medical aid station. It received casualties, both wounded and killed in action. Was a dead soldier less prayed for by family, friends, and church than a live one? Maybe the dead soldier had less faith? Possibly the family didn't have enough faith. Maybe the dead soldier had committed a grievous sin and death was the punishment. Possibly, there was a grievous sin committed by someone in the family and death of the soldier was the punishment. Maybe it was

MIRACLES: WHAT, WHY, AND HOW?

simply "God's will!" Faith, sin, and God's will are all used to explain the lack of divine intervention in extreme situations. It was while serving in Vietnam I definitely concluded that God was blamed for a lot of things that couldn't otherwise be explained. I also came to the conclusion that if God really willed these things, it was not a God in whom I believed. To believe that God willed the death of soldiers in Vietnam, I would have to believe God willed the war. God would have to will the war in order to will men and women to be killed in the war! Does your God box contain this kind of God? Although I speak of Vietnam because I served there, I would apply the same concept to any armed conflict since the beginning of history.

I should add a few words here about those who were not killed or maybe had narrow escapes from death or being wounded. Did God perform miracles to get them through unscathed, or at least alive? Were their prayers more sincere than those who suffered death or severe wounds? Is it possible they had more people praying for them, and those multiple prayers made a difference? Maybe they just had more faith and it pulled them through. Possibly it had nothing to do with faith or number of prayers. Maybe God had no need to punish them for some grievous infraction. Maybe it was just God's will for them to get through without injury or being killed. Some would say they made it because God had something else in mind for them to accomplish. I have to state I don't believe any of what I just said, any more than I believe those who didn't survive died because of not enough prayers, not enough faith, punishment for sin, or because it was God's will. The God in my box does not cause these things. They are part of a natural process in a world where humans have free choice. Those choices may lead to power, greed, or disaster. Others may try to stop the power, greed, or disaster and become victims in the process.

If God had the ability to feed the hungry with manna from heaven, why doesn't he take care of the famines in the world today? If God protected the Jewish people in biblical times, why did he allow the Holocaust? If we attribute supernatural powers to a supernatural deity, then we need to ask: why not more miracles? Why are miracles withheld in such critical situations that literally impact the lives of thousands of people? Why are so many thousands of lives filled with pain, tragedy, and sickness? If God is all-powerful, why do we have natural disasters that kill thousands of people and cause widespread destruction?

One expressed attitude throughout the Bible is one that believes if we need the supernatural deity to perform a miracle on our behalf, it will happen. There is an escape clause that goes along with the question. It is one I emphasize again and is held by many Christians, not just those of the fundamentalist persuasion. The answer goes back to my triad. If the miracle is not forthcoming, it is because the person did not have enough faith, the person was being punished for something (remember what Job's friends were telling him), or, the final copout, it is God's will.

Another one I hear occasionally associated with a tragedy claims God is testing the faith of those involved. This also could be said about the story of Job. This creates a magical view of a supernatural deity and life that promotes the belief biblical miracle stories are literal history. Discounted is the idea that miracle stories were religious myths which were told and retold and became exaggerated through years of oral transmission before being written down.

I will use the Moses stories to give two examples. Keep in mind Moses lived about 1250 BCE, give or take a few years. He was without doubt a great hero to the Jewish people. Stories were told and retold about him, and it was probably at least 300 years before anything was written down. Do you think it might be possible the stories were exaggerated? Moses led the Israelites out of Egyptian bondage. He was their "Get Out of Jail" card. What was their first big obstacle? We have all heard of crossing the Red Sea. For those who have seen Cecil B. DeMille's depiction in the movie *The Ten Commandments*, it is an awesome, spectacular, and definitely miraculous event. I can still see the water dividing and the surging wall of water on each side of the dry land over which the escaping people walked. How close to what really happened is that scene? I doubt if there was any accuracy at all. If they went through the Red Sea, they went miles out of their way. The

MIRACLES: WHAT, WHY, AND HOW?

Red Sea is about twenty miles wide at its narrowest point. The story indicates they went through it overnight. Let's give them ten hours to do that. In that period of time they would have to average twelve miles per hour. That figures out to five-minute miles. I was a runner for years (not a fast one), and I never, ever got close to five-minute miles, and I was in excellent condition. The crossing story is impossible! We are talking about young and old, weak and strong, healthy and sick, male and female. It is also impossible if you consider the number of people who would have to cross in that period of time.

Now let us look at a logical explanation. First of all, the Hebrew refers to the body of water crossed as Yam Suph, which was translated into the words "Red Sea." Actually, the term probably would be better translated as "sea of reeds." My understanding is this area is not even identified with the Red Sea, but is a swampland north of what we know as the Gulf of Suez. This marshy area was covered with shallow water and appears to be less than twenty miles across. Twenty miles of marsh covered by shallow water being traversed by old, young, sick, and healthy men and women would still be a major undertaking. It would not be accomplished overnight, but at least they could cross it. The Egyptian Army, with armor, weapons, chariots, and horses, would get bogged down. So in one sense it was a miracle, or more accurately, a marvel! The important thing to them was they escaped. Because of what they had endured at the hands of the Egyptians, is it any wonder they believed God had rescued them?

Now look again at the time frame. It was another twelve generations before any of this was written. It is easy to see how the marvel became a miracle. After all, the Israelites were God's chosen people. He had delivered them, which again proved he was the one who could control nature.

They escaped! Then what? They spent years wandering in the desert and thinking they may have been better off staying in Egypt. So here we have another miracle story concerning Moses. What to eat? Simple, God through Moses provided manna to eat. I found some interesting information concerning manna. It is actually a sticky substance secreted by certain insects. The secretion forms into sweet drops the size of peas. These harden on the leaves of tamarisk plants overnight and fall off come morning. I read that Bedouin Arabs gather manna as part of their regular diet from May through July. I see nothing here indicating a supernatural deity interfering with the laws of nature. I will admit there may have been an unexplainable event happening here. It is difficult to visualize enough insects to provide the amount of daily manna it would take to feed all the Israelites. I also am not sure what they would have done from the end of July until the beginning of May, nine months later. I do see how the story being retold for twelve generations would become a miracle of God looking out for his chosen people through their great leader, Moses.

When I was a child in Sunday school, one of my favorite stories was the story of Jonah and the whale. It is a story even the biblically illiterate seem to know. It was a favorite because I was constantly trying to figure out how a person could live in a whale for three days. Don't ask me why this intrigued me more than other miracle stories in the Old Testament, but it did. I was almost disappointed when I learned there was no city of Nineveh at the time the book is believed to have been written. Reason eventually set in, and I realized I would never figure out how a man could survive in a fish for three days. It was impossible. Accepting that the story didn't say it was a whale, but a big fish, took away some of my mental imagery. Still today, most people think in terms of a whale. Religious artwork illustrating the story generally has the big fish looking very much like a whale. Instead of the story being one to prove God could do anything—a man living in a fish for three days—I realized there was a different lesson here. Many different lessons have been taught from the Jonah story, but the one that stood out for me was that you couldn't run from God. Such an explanation seems much more credible than a man in a fish for three days. This is another of those stories where what it means is much more important than if it really happened. I know, the fundamentalists still use the story as a literal illustration of the miraculous power of a supernatural deity. I am willing to let it be their problem and not mine. Can a person live in the

MIRACLES: WHAT, WHY, AND HOW?

belly of a big fish for three days? You decide.

It is important to keep in mind miracles have a place in most religions of the world. When persons become aware of the vastness of the universe and believe they are at the mercy of the forces of nature, it can become a scary scenario. That is exactly what happened down through the ages as humankind battled with the forces of nature. In order not to feel alone and at the mercy of the elements, a conviction developed that out there somewhere was a supernatural deity who was in control and would watch over them, intervening if necessary.

What happens when you take this supernatural deity, the concept of theism, out of the scenario? We see the kind of resistance, for example, that pushes against the concept of evolution. It is resistance that is most often present in the fundamentalists' brand of Christianity. What is the fear? Evolution is perceived as taking God out of the equation. If evolution is true and natural selection is the way things happen, where is the hand of God in this? Evolution has to be a miracle. Unacceptable is the idea the Bible doesn't say how the world was created, only pointing to the power behind it. To even suggest biblical miracle stories are not to be taken literally comes as a shock to some. It is scary, and may even anger them. If the miracles are not literally true, what happens to our security system? If there is no supernatural deity, where do we turn for help and protection? What happens to our prayers if there is no guy in the sky who will respond? He must be up there because we believe he is there, we believe he will come to our aid. We believe he will cure our health problems. We believe he will protect us from anyone who dares endanger us. We believe he will protect us while driving down the highway. We believe a soldier prayed for will be protected in battle. At least that is what a religious system headed by one who is infallible or has a sacred scripture inspired and inerrant would like you to believe. The truth of the matter is it doesn't happen that way. But, you say, we have miracle stories in scripture that say miracles do happen. Using scripture to prove scripture is not my idea of how to arrive at fact. To even suggest that miracle stories in the Bible are not literally true is nothing short of heresy to some believers.

GOD IN A BOX

I do believe unexplainable events happen in our world, but I stop short of calling them miracles. At the same time I have no problem with those who refer to them as miracles. I just prefer to call them unexplainable events. I believe some events classified as miracles in biblical times could happen today. There are those who believe many miracles happened in biblical times but cannot happen today. You have to remember, I don't believe many of the miracles listed in scripture are literal. For example, I don't believe the sun stood still in biblical times, so I don't believe it could stand still in our time. If that happened, it would truly be a miracle. On the other hand, I do believe there were unexplainable healings that happened in biblical times. Again, I choose to call them unexplainable events. I believe the same thing about unexplained healings that take place in our day and age. Again, I call them unexplainable events or marvels, not miracles. We don't know all the factors at work in the mind and body that are able to cause remission of disease or healing of a health problem. Herbert Benson, M.D., in his book *Beyond The Relaxation Response*, said, "...I believe most of us have little idea how great our individual potential or 'performance ceiling' is, both physically and mentally. If you truly believe in your personal philosophy or religious faith—if you are committed, mind and soul, to your world view—you may well be capable of achieving remarkable feats of mind and body that many only speculate about."

If we go to the earliest writings of the New Testament, which I have pointed out are the writings of Paul, you will not find any recorded miracles, unless you count Paul's belief that God had raised Jesus from the dead. Paul's miraculous conversion is not even recorded by him. That story of Paul's conversion comes out of the book of Acts and may or may not be an accurate account. As Paul doesn't mention it, I do regard it with suspicion.

The first miracle stories are recorded in the gospel of Mark, and then follow in the other gospels. Why do you think miracles stories started appearing in the stories about Jesus? We have to keep in mind his followers had a difficult time finding words explaining what he meant to them and how they perceived his impact on the world. One

MIRACLES: WHAT, WHY, AND HOW?

way of explaining his impact is to attach miracle stories that took place during his time with them. That is not too farfetched when we remember these writers were influenced by Jewish tradition and wrote from that perspective. Just look at the Old Testament and you will see how much belief was present and used to show how God had power over creation. If God was perceived as intervening in the world on behalf of the Israelites, and Jesus was the Son of God, wouldn't he have the same powers? I believe the followers of Jesus used miracle stories to show how the power of God was working through the life and ministry of Jesus. Again, they were trying to express a powerful internal presence of God they experienced through Jesus. That experience was inexpressible by language alone unless they used the language of their religious tradition to explain his impact. The language of their religious tradition was filled with miracle stories; thus miracle stories were told about Jesus. This is not to say they were using the words to prove Jesus could overpower laws of nature. They were telling the stories to prove God was in Jesus. They were using words to show the God of the Old Testament—who they believed had control over nature—was now being manifested in a new way in the life of Jesus. God had been the source of deliverance to the Jewish people in the Old Testament. The New Testament stories proclaim Jesus—sent from God—is their source of deliverance.

In the chapter on Jesus, I did not talk about Jesus and healing miracles. You can surmise from what I have already written that I believe there are unexplainable healings by Jesus. I put much more credibility in something happening to people because of their encounter with Jesus than I do in nature miracle stories told about Jesus. The miracle stories surrounding Jesus continue to impact people in this generation. Jesus healed by touch and command, and there is no shortage of people today who claim to heal in the name of Jesus in the same fashion. *Faith that Heals: Stories of God's Love,* a compilation of interviews with hundreds of Christians in the Columbus, South Carolina, area deals with this type of healing. The book tells about many different kinds of healings experienced by people. Some stories related by the individual telling the story were accounts of having healed others. Are any of these provable or disprovable as miracles? Probably not, but I would say for every story told, the storyteller believed what they were telling to be an absolutely true and miraculous story. I will not make a comment either way—I wasn't there.

I believe there are still unexplainable remissions and healings of sickness, and these are not limited to the Christian religion. It can happen by ministrations of a witch doctor, medicine man, faith healer, or whatever other name you want to give one who seems to bring about change in a person's mental or physical condition. Not all are perceived to be brought about by offering prayers to a supernatural deity who can do direct intervention if the prayers are sincere, the faith is strong, and the supernatural deity is so inclined. Isn't it interesting that if there is healing, God gets the credit? If there isn't healing, who gets the blame? Let's review my triad on that. If there is no healing, it is because of not enough faith, being punished for some sin, or because it is simply God's will! Whatever the outcome might be, it is always a win-win situation for God. But for us, any part of the triad may make us losers.

Reviewing an actual event may be helpful in understanding blame or credit. On January 2, 2006, there was an explosion in the Sago Mine in Tallmansville, West Virginia. Thirteen miners were trapped twenty feet below the surface. How could they possibly survive without oxygen? Then a miracle occurred. It was reported twelve of the men had been found alive. There was much celebration at the Sago Baptist Church. The governor of West Virginia even went so far as to announce it was a miracle and told people from then on they needed to believe in miracles. It is interesting to me why that miracle did not include the thirteenth man. No one even asked that question. Television coverage showed people who attributed the rescue to divine intervention. The religious phrases "Thank you, God," "Thank you, Jesus," and "Praise God" were heard repeatedly. Then a few hours later everything changed. Only one miner was barely alive and twelve were dead! The thankfulness for a miracle was replaced by anger and hate. I don't remember anyone praising God for the one who was still alive.

You see, it is my belief that most times in situations of this type,

MIRACLES: WHAT, WHY, AND HOW?

believers' prayers are unanswered far more often than they are answered. Why would that be? Is it because the people don't have enough faith, punishment for sin is involved, or because what happens is God's will? You decide.

Moving on, we need to look deeper at how sickness was viewed in the first century. They had none of the medical or scientific knowledge we have today. The words "germ" and "virus" were certainly unknown. There was certainly no understanding of heart problems, cancer, tuberculosis, or a myriad of other diseases we know about today. Sickness was generally understood as something that happened to someone who had angered God or, in other words, had sinned. Remember the event in John 9:2? The disciples certainly portrayed the prevalent thought of the day when they asked, *"Rabbi, who sinned this man or his parents, that he was born blind?"* There was no knowledge of mental illness or epilepsy. The New Testament viewed both as being caused by demon possession (Mark 1:23-26, 9:17-27, Matthew 8:28-32).

Is it any wonder if sickness was due to one's sins, or if God willed things to happen, you needed to be very careful to offer the correct prayers and offer adequate sacrifices to quiet the wrath of an angry or offended God? That ancient way of viewing sickness as punishment for sin even had a carryover into the twentieth century. It was a part of some prayer books until revised in the late 1900s.

Today we live in a world of technology that absolutely could not have been imagined in the first century. Imagine we had a time machine able to go back and bring a first century citizen to the twenty-first century for a week. When he got back to the first century, can you imagine the tales he would tell? Talk about miracles, he would have thousands of them. They would range from medical technology to electronics with a lot of stuff in between. Look at the miracles he could tell just about modes of transportation—airplanes, cars, space travel, ships. His knowledge base would be such that the only way he could explain them would be to call them miracles. He would most likely be considered to be demon-possessed to be telling some of the tales he would relate, and he would probably become an outcast. To us, the things we have are not considered miracles. I would say much we have could be considered marvels of modern technology. Today we have vaccines, radiation, chemotherapy, surgical techniques, and antibiotics that would mystify even our own parents. I am absolutely amazed by the advances I have seen in my lifetime. Modern technology has extended our life span in a way that defies what would have been thought possible just a few years ago, let alone generations ago. It might even be said no one dies of natural causes anymore. I do sometimes wonder if this is all good. Sometimes what we have done is not to create an extension to the quality of life. but to complicate and extend the process of dying. We extend life in ways that can become detrimental instead of helpful.

Have you ever seen a patient with no cognitive recognition of anything around him or her? Such a patient may be curled up in a fetal position, fed through a stomach tube, turned to help prevent bedsores, and with a dire prognosis of never improving. What is the quality of life and the medical miracle in such a situation? It is almost as if death seems to be viewed as losing a battle rather than as a natural part of the progression, which begins at birth and ends at death. Being born is terminal; no one gets out of this world alive. For some reason, many individuals still seem to think being here in any condition is better than not being here. The sad part is we sometimes make that decision for others when that would not be their wish at all! This may be especially true when a family is unwilling to let go of a loved one. We fear euthanasia, but refuse to give a suffering, terminal patient the right to end it all.

Now back to healings by Jesus. The question remains, did Jesus actually do healing miracles or did his followers tell these stories to prove he really was the expected Messiah? I vote on the side of a little of both. In the gospels of Matthew and Luke, the question is posed by John the Baptist as to whether or not Jesus was the one to fulfill messianic expectations. Jesus replies by paraphrasing some verses from Isaiah 35, *"...the blind receive sight, the lame walk, the lepers are cleansed, the deaf hear, the dead are raised, and the poor have good news brought to them."* (Matthew 11:4-5). What is added here and not in Isaiah is the phrase

MIRACLES: WHAT, WHY, AND HOW?

"the dead are raised." Did Jesus actually say these things? We will never be able to prove it one way or the other, but probably not. There is also disagreement among scholars as to whether these events actually took place. These stories could very well be told to explain what the coming of Jesus meant to them, rather than actual literal happenings. They could be based on events that happened and through the process of oral tradition grew over the years as they were told and retold to emphasize what people experienced through Jesus. Again, I say I am not willing to completely discount the healing stories. This is primarily due to the reading I have done pointing to modern time's accounts of healings that have taken place in different parts of the world and have no adequate explanation. Some of these healings have happened to people with no relationship to Jesus or any type of religious faith.

There is little doubt Jesus was viewed as a healer and exorcist. There are too many stories in the New Testament to discount this aspect of his ministry. What actually happened in those stories may be questioned, but something happened that was perceived as extraordinary. Even Josephus, the Jewish historian I mentioned earlier, wrote that Jesus was a "doer of mighty deeds." Marcus J. Borg, in a book co-authored with N. T. Wright, *The Meaning of Jesus Two Visions*, does state Jesus' healings were probably based on some history remembered, and referred to them as paranormal healings. He says, "I very deliberately refer to Jesus' healings as paranormal, meaning unusual, alongside the normal, or beyond the ordinary." Borg also thinks they were probably not psychosomatic or miracles wrought by supernatural intervention. He further states, "Inexplicable and remarkable things do happen, involving processes that we do not understand."

Paranormal would be a great explanation for many healings I have read about. I have some disagreement on the psychosomatic claim. I believe some healings can be attributed to psychosomatic issues. In any case, I believe these are not to be considered as healings brought about by a supernatural deity. I no longer accept the idea of a supernatural deity intervening in life. For those who do, I raise the question again, how do you explain the non-interventions? My preference is still to refer to what some call miracles as unexplainable events, not miracles. Almost daily, we hear about things that are unexplainable and often quite remarkable. I would say they just involve some process still beyond our understanding.

In the New Testament, healing was recorded as a major component of the ministry of Jesus. To heal would certainly portray Jesus as being one who had great compassion. It is amazing what compassion for one in need can do. It could even bring about a paranormal or psychosomatic healing. When I was on active duty in the Army, we had a psychiatrist talk to a group of chaplains about problem soldiers. These were soldiers who always seemed to be in trouble and whose lives appeared to be all messed up. This could be due to bad decisions, a horrible childhood, or some type of traumatic event. He said, in spite of the problems faced by some of these soldiers, they turned their lives around. I asked him how he explained a turnaround, and he answered with two words: "Somebody cared." Has there ever been someone who cared more than Jesus? Showing love and compassion as Jesus showed love and compassion can bring wholeness to people. And how does that happen? I don't know, any more than I can explain other paranormal or psychosomatic events. The power is not in the explanation of the event but in seeing what can happen.

During my ministry in the military, I led a number of different groups that some would call therapy groups, but I simply called them growth groups. One of these groups was a couple's group. It included couples who were having marital difficulties as well as couples who just wanted to improve their marriage. During one session, one of the wives was very disturbed and strung out. She felt as if life was pushing in on all sides of her and she had no place to go. The group talked and shared with her their personal experiences and how they had coped with issues. Nothing helped ease her distress. I had been reading about the power of touch and how energy can flow from one person to another. I had also witnessed this in demonstrations in some classes I had taken. I asked the wife if she would be willing for members of the group to hold her and gently rock her. She said she was ready to try anything. I

MIRACLES: WHAT, WHY, AND HOW?

had her lie down on the carpet with four members of the group kneeling on each side of her. They slipped their hands under her body and slowly raised her off the carpet. Then I asked them to rock her gently back and forth for a short period of time. Then they lowered her slowly back to the carpet. The room was so quiet you could hear a pin drop. The members who had lifted her moved back to their chairs, and she continued to lie on the carpet without saying anything. After a few moments, she spoke and her voice was entirely different. The best way to describe it is to say it was a calm voice, rather than one filled with anxiety. She shared that she had never had a feeling like she felt when being lifted and rocked. She described it as a feeling of being secure and cared for by those around her.

We then processed the event as a group. Several things of note were revealed. The lifters said they could feel something going from their hands into her body when they lifted and rocked. They described it as heat and energy flow. The wife said that she could feel the heat and energy flow into her body, and it was the most soothing and calming feeling she had ever experienced. Another item of note was the general mental feeling of the lifters. They said they had never felt such a sense of caring and compassion for another person as they did when lifting and rocking. The wife said she felt like the people really cared about her during the process, and she didn't want to ever lose that feeling. What happened in the process? I really can't explain it, other than to say the compassion of the group was somehow made very real to the wife and changed how she felt. I might add she continued to express a feeling of being cared for throughout the remainder of the group sessions.

Have you heard of the butterfly effect? It is a theory stating the flapping of a butterfly's wings, or the wings of any insect for that matter, can contribute to a chain of events that could even result in some type of severe weather pattern someplace else. Think hurricane, tornado, or even a tsunami. It is tied to the idea that the movement of one particle could affect the movement of a different particle thousands of miles away. Now, place that theory with actions of human beings. There are Nobel Prize-winning scientists who proclaim a multiple-worlds theory.

GOD IN A BOX

This theory ties in with the butterfly effect, only with broader ramifications. My choices in this universe may have some type of effect on an alternative universe somewhere out there, one of which I have absolutely no awareness.

I believe there could be a relationship between the butterfly effect, quantum physics, and the string theory. With my limited understanding of it all, I have arrived at some conclusions about life in general. String theory does proclaim there are at least eight additional dimensions of reality of which we have no conscious awareness. Dr. Michio Kaku has claimed there are eleven different dimensions in our universe. Dr. Kaku is an American theoretical physicist, and the Henry Semat Professor of Theoretical Physics in the City College of New York and City University of New York. He is also a futurist and popularizer of science. He has written two *New York Times* Best Sellers, *Physics of the Impossible* (2008) and *Physics of the Future* (2011). He may be familiar to some of you as he has appeared on numerous television shows as well as having hosted television specials for BBC-TV, the Discovery Channel, the History Channel, and the Science Channel. I have listed some of his credentials to show he is not just a fly-by-night physicist.

However many dimensions there may be, it seems no one has been able to communicate with any of those dimensions. If string theory is true, a criticism of his theory is if no one has been able to communicate with those dimensions, how can we even know they exist, and how can we know there are eleven? Lack of current proof to me does not equate to nonexistence. This would not be the first theory of science not proven and later discovered to be true. We need to look at a few examples.

In 1633, during the Inquisition, Galileo was brought to trial for heresy. He was found guilty and condemned by the Holy Roman Catholic Church for "vehement suspicion of heresy." This is the same Galileo who has been credited with the birth of modern science. Albert Einstein went so far as to call him the father of modern science. Finally in 1992, Pope John Paul II expressed regret on how Galileo had been treated. The announcement was seen as formally and publically clearing Galilee of any wrongdoing. With every new discovery, there are

MIRACLES: WHAT, WHY, AND HOW?

changes beyond current thought.

The ancient commonly held view that sin or devil possession caused disease was discounted with the discovery and control of germs. Aristotle believed it was spontaneous generation that caused aphids to come out of morning dew on plants. He also held the same theory caused fleas to come out of putrid matter. The one really hard to accept is his belief that mice came from dirty hay! How many years before those theories were overcome?

Louis Pasteur was one of two men who had a tremendous impact on the medical world. Pasteur proved airborne microbes were the cause of disease. His career showed how conservative the medical establishment was at the time. Dr. Joseph Lister did not discover a new drug, but he did make the link between the lack of cleanliness in hospitals and deaths after operations. For this reason, he is known as the "Father of Antiseptic Surgery." These are examples of things that had been discounted and later proven to be true. A theory yet to be proven does not mean it should be readily discounted.

A recent issue concerns the Higgs boson, sometimes referred to as "the God Particle." It is called "the God Particle" because some say it is what caused "the Big Bang." The Big Bang is said to be what created our universe billions of years ago. Not everyone believes calling it the God Particle is a good idea, saying the Higgs boson had absolutely nothing to do with the Big Bang. Higgs bosons, existing all around us, are supposed to help us understand how something can come from nothing. The Higgs boson explains why particles have mass. Proof of its existence would assist in explaining how anything at all exists. The Higgs boson is named after Peter Higgs. He is one of six physicists who proposed in 1964 that such a particle existed but had no proof of it. Guess what? On March 14, 2013, the Higgs boson was tentatively confirmed to exist. The confirmation came through experiments using the Large Hadron Collider, a particle accelerator in Switzerland. Almost fifty years after they proposed the theory, Peter Higgs and Francois Englert were awarded the 2013 Nobel Prize in physics for their work in explaining how matter formed after the Big Bang. It has been suggested this was a one-in-a-trillion event. I believe it is unwise to say something is not true or doesn't exist because it has not yet been seen or proven. The opposite would also be true. It is unwise to say unequivocally that something is true or does exist if it hasn't been seen or proven.

Again I was sidetracked. I wanted to give some examples showing that because a thing has not been seen or believed to be true does not mean it won't be seen or proven to be true at a future time. I believe there is a connectedness between all of life. Somehow, in some way, we are all connected. Is it possible for this connectedness to take place in one of those eleven dimensions of which we are unaware? It appears to me to be a reasonable possibility. Don't ask me to explain it—I can't—but I like to think I see it in events. As I illustrated in the story about the woman in my couple's group, I believe energy can flow from one person (or persons) to another. This energy can be felt as genuine caring and may even have healing qualities. I can't prove it happens, neither can you disprove it. I know energy flowing from one human being to another seems more viable as a source of healing than intervention from some supernatural theistic being who resides somewhere beyond the sky. Based on string theory, is it necessary to limit energy flow to only those individuals we can reach out and touch? Maybe the time will come when we will have an answer to that, not speculative but factual! Maybe the God all around us can move freely through all eleven dimensions. Maybe in moving through these dimensions, God interacts with the world in ways we do not understand. Maybe the results of some of these interactions are what some call miracles. Can this be proven? It most certainly cannot be proven with our present knowledge. Can it be disproven? Again, no. Is it further from where we are in science today to finding the eleven dimensions than it was from the three-tiered view of the universe to where we are today? That poses another one of those questions that cannot be answered.

In what manner might the dimensions work in our lives? The question always arises concerning what happens with intercessory prayer. There have been several studies conducted to measure the effectiveness of intercessory prayer. The results are not conclusive. Some of the

MIRACLES: WHAT, WHY, AND HOW?

controlled studies have shown no change in those prayed for and those who were not included in prayer. Other controlled studies have shown improvement or quicker recovery of those who were the recipients of intercessory prayers. These were studies in which the recipients were unaware they were receiving such prayers. I'm willing to accept improvement was present in the recipients of intercessory prayers. What I am unwilling to accept is that improvement was a result of intervention by a supernatural theistic being who heard the prayers and responded. How can it be proven supernatural deity intervention was the reason for improvement? It is just as possible that our connectedness in some unknown dimension (one of the eleven) was the reason for improvement. This cannot be proven either, but is more acceptable to my way of perceiving cause and effect. There is one thing that bothers me about studies proving prayers bring about an intervention from a supernatural theistic deity. If the supernatural theistic deity is compassionate and loving, why did this being have to wait for intercessory prayer before intervening in the life of the sick person?

Are there other examples of intercessory prayers bringing about a miracle of healing? It depends on how you choose to view it. There are so many variables in what can take place in the human mind and body, it is impossible to prove a direct cause and effect. Can you prove that intercessory prayer got the supernatural deity's attention? Philip Yancey, in his book *Prayer: Does It Make any Difference?* poses some valid questions, such as, "Does a person with many praying friends stand a better chance of physical healing than one who also has cancer but with only a few people praying for her?" and, "Does the sick woman who happens to have praying friends stand a better chance for recovery than an equally deserving person who does not?" These are questions that cannot be ignored. If you answer yes to either question, then you are describing a God in whom I cannot believe. That is not the God in my God box.

Why does God need prayers of intercession before he can intercede on behalf of a sick person? How can you know what happened would not have happened anyway? Can you prove that a positive outcome was not due to energy released through the care and concern of others? If the mind actually occupies an "out there" dimension, is it also possible that somewhere out there is a field of consciousness in which we are all connected? Dr. Amit Goswami, a theoretical nuclear physicist at the University of Oregon Institute of Theoretical Science, said, "If ordinary people really knew that consciousness and not matter is the link that connects us with each other and the world, then their views about war and peace, environmental pollution, social justice, religious values, and all other human endeavors would change radically." Note that he includes religious values in his statement. If there are different layers or dimensions to our universe (string theory) and if in some way we are connected together in a field or a different dimension, is it possible that in some way this connectedness is what creates the energy of intercessory prayer (a religious value)? This is entirely different from saying we changed God's mind and God intervened.

Should we quit offering intercessory prayers if there is no supernatural deity available to act on them? If you are praying to somehow manipulate the supernatural deity to bring about your desired outcome, you probably should just as well cease. If, as I explained above, you believe there is a type of connectedness between all of us, then by no means stop! We don't know what kind of energy we release when we offer this type of prayer. Intercessory prayer can be a symbol of our need to care for each other. I think caring is what Jesus did and what we are called upon to do. Intercessory prayer is too often seen as an expression of a need to believe there is a power out there we can count on to protect us and work a miracle if we need one. What does it say about the deity if the miracle is not granted? I know, when it doesn't happen refer back to my triad—not enough faith, punishment for sin, or God's will. I close this section with a question. If God is love and God is all-powerful, why wouldn't God want to intervene without being asked? You decide.

While I was working on this chapter I was diagnosed with epithelioid hemangioendothelioma, a very rare form of cancer. We were in Arizona, visiting family, but our home is in Kansas. I decided to start

MIRACLES: WHAT, WHY, AND HOW?

treatment in Arizona before we returned home. We are part of a very active Sunday school class in Kansas, and very supportive of any class member who has a problem. One aspect of the class is a prayer chain. A name and request are given to the person handling the prayer chain, and an e-mail or telephone call goes out to all members of the class to pray for that person. I wanted the class to be aware of the situation, but was hesitant to make contact because I knew many of the prayers would be for an intervention from the supernatural deity to heal me. As that goes contrary to my own belief, I did not want to be seen as hypocritical with such a request. I decided not to make contact with the class but did decide to let our pastor, a good friend, know about the cancer. The result was that he notified the class, and I found myself in the situation I had hoped to avoid. I received many cards, and e-mails, and prayers, which I did appreciate. Some of the class believes much the same way as I do, and their messages had special significance to me. One simply said words to the effect of "best wishes." I liked that.

Am I worse off because I didn't accept the idea the prayers would have an influence on a supernatural deity, accepted by many members of the class as God? I don't think so. Whatever will be will be, not in the sense of fatalism, or that it is already all predetermined. What I do mean is with medical knowledge, my own inner resources, and support of friends (that connectedness through an unknown dimension), whatever will be will be. I also have to add that with what I believe about us all being connected in some way, any prayer offered up could possibly connect—not to an intervening God but to me, and would be supportive. Did I feel the support of the class members and other friends not members of the class? Yes I did! Are there miracles? Again, that will be up to you. You decide.

6

THE HEREAFTER: HEAVEN, HELL, PURGATORY OR…?

Whatever else you may think about the hereafter, one thing cannot be denied. You have to die to get there. There is a song with the words "Everybody wants to go to heaven but nobody wants to die." I am amused by Woody Allen's response when asked some questions about death. He replied, "I'm not afraid of dying—I just don't want to be there when it happens!" If you haven't grasped the reality yet, I have news for you: you are going to die. Depending on your belief system, it could be debated whether or not heaven will be your final destination. Whatever the destination, it's the prospect of dying that has tremendous influence on how we view the hereafter. Our greatest fear may not be the reality of dying as much as the thought of no longer being. Norman Cousins, in his book *The Celebration of Life—A Dialogue on Immortality and Infinity*, says, "…the quest for immortality may actually reflect the inherent desire in man for the indefinite perpetuation of self." What is it like to not be? I like to tell people that I am prepared to die, but I am not ready to die. Do I fear "not being" if that is the result of my death? I do not, simply because if that is the end result, I won't know anything about it anyway. My greatest concern is dying before my spouse. I have prided myself in taking care of her through the many

THE HEREAFTER: HEAVEN, HELL, PURGATORY OR…?

years of our marriage. I want to continue to take care of her until her demise. I don't want her to have to deal with my demise. That's an extra I threw in, and you can do with it what you want.

Another important fact is that most of what you have been told about the hereafter cannot be proven! Now isn't that a rather bold statement? The only thing I think might be provable about the hereafter is being physically dead. It is like being pregnant—you either are or you are not!

With that delightful introduction let us move on to some questions. When did you first hear about life after death? What did you hear about it? Where was life after death located? How was it described? How did you get there? Why was it important? How has your thinking changed from how you answered the previous questions? My guess is for most of you, the answers in the past to the above questions are rather close to where you are still caught today. The hereafter is something about which almost everyone has questions. It is also something about which most people are hesitant to rock the boat by asking too many questions. Our need for security is such that we would rather find comfort in what we have heard about the hereafter and like, rather than question if what we have heard is valid or provable. Remember, earlier I said in a survey a majority of people questioned said they were Christians to make sure they went to heaven. They are Christians to provide for eternal security.

Maurice S. Rawlings, M.D., in his book *To Hell and Back,* quotes Dr. E. V. Hill, then pastor of Mt. Zion Missionary Baptist Church in Los Angeles, California. The quote underlines what I have said. Dr. Hill had a classic sermon titled "Why I Am a Christian." His first and most important point was *"I DON'T WANT TO GO TO HELL!"* For those fundamentalists who believe in a literal heaven and a literal hell, it provides fire insurance. It would have been interesting to ask them to describe to what kind of heaven they were going—or to what kind of hell they were escaping. I can assure you for some it would fall close to what they heard as a child. You would probably hear some mention of pearly gates and golden streets. The downside would probably have something to do with fire and devils or the big Satan. For others, heaven might be some vague something out there, but something they don't want to take a chance of missing. Any chance someone might refer to it as just another dimension of which we are unaware while alive? That's possible, but doubtful. So where do we get our images of the hereafter? Did they just suddenly spurt forth out of some preacher's mouth? Most likely some of our images come from that very source. And what was the preacher's source? That would be an interesting one to track down. Also interesting is to listen to a preacher talk about the hereafter (generally heaven) in a funeral, compared to discussing it in a conversation. Platitudes are often used in a funeral to soothe the grief of the mourners. But, can those platitudes be backed up with facts? I daresay most of them cannot.

If we look at Jewish history, a belief in an afterlife as presently understood has not always been a part of Jewish religious belief. There was a type of existence after death, but it was in an underworld of ghosts and shadowy figures and had no hopes associated with it. It was a shadowy world called Sheol. It was believed that God had no control over Sheol. Psalm 88:4-5 says, *"I am counted among those who go down to the Pit; I am like those who have no help, like those forsaken among the dead, like the slain that lie in the grave, like those whom you remember no more, for they are cut off from your hand."* God was believed to be infinite and eternal, but human beings were fragile and had nothing eternal about them. Your hereafter was how you lived on as a memory in the community. Your hereafter was in the heirs you propagated while living. The point to remember is belief in the hereafter as presently viewed has not always been a part of the Judeo/Christian heritage.

As we move forward in Jewish thought, we see the development of the idea God was also in control of Sheol. Psalm 139:7-8 provides strong words to support this: *"Where can I go from your spirit? Or where can I flee from your presence? If I ascend to heaven, you are there; if I make my bed in Sheol, you are there."* A ray of hope was cast, proclaiming that maybe Sheol was not the ultimate end. The Psalmist says in 49:15, *"But God will ransom my soul from the power of Sheol, for he will receive me."*

THE HEREAFTER: HEAVEN, HELL, PURGATORY OR...?

Thinking developed that Sheol might even have rewards and punishments administered to its inhabitants. From there it was just a short step to the hope that life could be restored again in full.

Having significant impact on the hope of life after death was the development of personal religion as experiencing an inner relationship between the soul of a person and God. This was quite different from early Jewish religious thought, which had religion as a primary focus on the group or tribe, not on the individual.

Another ingredient that needs to be added to this mix was the development of Jewish expectations of a future Messianic Age. This age would right all the wrongs suffered by the Jewish people. Justice would be done. But what do you do about the already dead, those already in Sheol? How would justice be done for them? Only one conclusion would work. The dead would be brought back to life. This was seen as a bodily resuscitation back to life on Earth. This would result in justice for those who suffered, rewards for the just. It would also result in judgment upon those who caused the suffering, punishment for the unjust. If it didn't happen in this life, it would happen in the resurrected life.

There were some strong influences on the development of the afterlife in Jewish thinking. One of these influences would be a concept borrowed from the Persian religion. After all, they were captives and under Persian influence for many years. We can see some major areas where Judaism and Zoroastrianism are similar. The similarities are evident because of the influence of Zoroastrianism. Both held to a separation of the righteous and the evil at the time of death. This separation would result in a blessed time for the righteous and a miserable time for the evil ones until a general resurrection of the dead, both righteous and evil, all at once. The final point of agreement was the belief in a last judgment with eternal consequences. Significant development of this thinking took place between the Old and New Testament periods. What it certainly produced was a sense of hope that had not been present before in quite the same way.

New developments were also taking place in concepts of Sheol. Of particular significance was the book of Enoch, written about two centuries B.C.E. If you can't find it in your Bible, it is part of the Apocrypha. The author divides Sheol into four different categories, two for the good people and two for the bad people. Starting with the place for the bad, this area contains the evil people who have died. They are having a tough time being constantly tormented while awaiting the resurrection. At the resurrection, they will receive the final pronouncements of their sentences of punishment. Another area is for evil people who have died and have already received their sentences. Unfortunately for them, there will be no resurrection, and there is no second chance. They must already be in hell or wherever their sentences have sent them. There are two areas for people who died and were considered good. There is an area for the moderately or average good people. I don't know the criteria for being moderate or average. The positive side is they are just waiting to receive their reward come judgment day. The last is the best category of all. In that waiting area reside all the very faithful or saintly. They must really stand out in some way to get to that level. There they enjoy perpetual paradise until the resurrection on the last day. After that it is on to eternal blessedness. Could someone tell me what would consist of a perpetual paradise? Following that, can someone describe what would be eternal blessedness?

Sheol for the Jews became intermediate, and in some ways preparatory, ending at the judgment day with the pronouncements of rewards and punishments. This is not too far removed from the thinking of Greek cults. Hades to them was a sort of holding place where souls were punished and corrected until they achieved goodness sufficient to allow the soul to ascend to God. It is my understanding that this idea of Sheol was carried over and influenced the Roman Catholic concept of purgatory. The most important item to take from this period is that death is no longer seen as the end; rather, in some way and in some fashion, there will be a future life. This future life could result in punishment or reward. If you were oppressed, you probably looked forward to when God would even the playing field.

There are references in the New Testament that some people interpret as in support of Jesus believing in an afterlife. When questioned by

THE HEREAFTER: HEAVEN, HELL, PURGATORY OR...?

the Sadducees—who didn't believe in the resurrection—about whose wife would the woman be who had been married a number of times, Jesus basically replied the question was not relevant, but in heaven they are like angels. (Matthew 22:23-33). Jesus was definitely a product of the beliefs of his time, but does that prove there is a heaven? If taken as proof, does that explain what it is like? Another passage used to support the belief of an afterlife comes from Jesus. In the gospel of John, Jesus says to his disciples, *"In my Father's house there are many dwelling places. If it were not so, would I have told you that I go to prepare a place for you?"* (John 14:2). My intent is not to prove or disprove whether Jesus believed in an afterlife. If there are many dwelling places, what are they like? You won't find any descriptions in these or any other words of Jesus.

Some will cite the book of Revelation as proof there is an afterlife and what it will be like. I am not willing to go there. Keep in mind, Revelation was written in a code to Christians of the first century concerning issues they faced in their time. Revelation no more describes a literal ending of the world than Genesis describes the literal beginning of the world. I just committed heresy again. If any fundamentalist got this far in the book, they know for sure where I am headed. I wonder if asbestos suits will be available?

If we explore other religions, we do find differences in what people believe about an afterlife. If you are a Muslim, you go straight to heaven. If you are a Muslim martyr, you have seventy-two virgins waiting for you. I assume that means if you are male. What is waiting for you if you are a female martyr? If you are a Hindu, you will be reincarnated. You will keep returning in a different body until you have reached that level of perfection which is the goal of each new life cycle. If you are an Orthodox Jew, you believe the righteous will be raised to a new resurrected body in a future general resurrection. Many Christians are not aware of this about the Orthodox Jewish faith. If you are a Buddhist, you just become one with the universe, and you retain no individuality. Most of the ancient peoples believed in some type of life after death; a resurrection was just not part of that belief.

GOD IN A BOX

What do people in the twenty-first century believe when they talk about life after death? There are those who believe at death there is complete annihilation of the person. There are some, like Hindus, who believe in reincarnation. General George Patton is not twenty-first century, but he was a proponent of reincarnation. The actress Shirley MacLaine is a present-day advocate of reincarnation. Is she an expert who can talk about reincarnation? It depends on what kind of expert you want. I quote her because she has very strong opinions about the subject. She is also probably one of the better known advocates of reincarnation. In her book, *I'm Over All That,* she shares her thoughts on reincarnation and reveals several past lives she believes she's had. "Probably one of the reasons why reincarnation makes sense to me is because I understand how each one of us is so many people. …When one understands karma, reincarnation—physical re-embodiment of the soul—is paramount. …The soul lives on and the learning of self continues."

Her book goes into much more detail about her past lives and what she experienced. Do you agree with her? Probably not, but can you prove her wrong? I would say definitely not. I want us to keep in mind that just because we don't believe something doesn't mean we can prove it to be false. On the other hand, we also need to keep in mind the opposite. Just because we believe something doesn't mean we can prove it to be true! This is one of the things that feeds my agnostic view towards many things. Being able and willing to say "I don't know" is very often the most honest answer, and one that I am not bothered to use. Regardless of where you stand, reincarnation is one of the beliefs supporting some type of afterlife.

There are some who hold a belief similar to Buddhists. They believe we are in some way absorbed into the greater world of space and matter. One of the messages left after the tragic death of Princess Diana read, "I did not leave you at all. I am still with you. I am in the sun and in the wind. I am even in the rain. I did not die, I am with you all." There are some Christians who hold to this concept. They believe the concept of ongoing life as part of the greater universe is what traditional teachings

THE HEREAFTER: HEAVEN, HELL, PURGATORY OR…?

about the immortality of the soul are all about.

We also need to include more traditional concepts. There are those who strongly believe being absent from the body is to be present with God. No explanation as to where this will be. Jesus told the thief on the cross that on that day he would be with him in Paradise. No explanation is given of what Paradise is or where we find it. Another strong belief is that at death we are reunited with our loved ones somewhere "up there." Note it is generally "up there," the location being greatly influenced by the old three-tier view of the universe. Remember, heaven is in the third tier or somewhere above the three tiers. For me, life after death is a manifestation of mankind's need to believe there is continued survival in some way, not extinction at the time of death. We cannot conceive of not being. What can keep us from extinction or "non-being" at death? For me, the answer is life after death, whatever that form of existence might be.

I want to take a look at some other popular Christian concepts concerning life after death. Have you ever heard of the phrase "A land flowing with milk and honey"? Do you know the origin of the phrase? It can be traced back to early history of the Hebrew people. When the Children of Israel were wandering in the desert, such a land was the dream in the hearts and minds of the people. In early Christianity, this phrase was taken out of context and built upon until it became a symbol of heaven. Heaven became a place where all needs are met.

If you have ever attended a Christian funeral, it is almost impossible to not have heard of heaven as a place where there would be "no sorrow, no sadness, no separation, and no death." This is a loose paraphrasing of Revelation 21:4. This points to a need to have some sense of connectivity with loved ones. We hurt because of the separation, so we convince ourselves the separation is only temporary. Clergy like to emphasis this one. It is a great way to bring comfort to the survivors. "Things are bad now, but never fear, you will see your loved ones again over there." I haven't heard any good explanations of "over there," except as already mentioned it is generally "up there." It seems quite natural for the grief stricken to dream of a place where they will be united with family and friends. Have you ever tried to take that thinking to its logical conclusion? When you arrive "over there," or "up there," or wherever, have you ever considered what role you will have, what age your body will be? How will a baby who died appear? Will you be a parent, a child, or a grandparent? If reunited with your parents as a child, how does that affect your reuniting with your children as a parent? If we are just some kind of vaporous being floating around in some other dimension, what difference does family association make? Interesting questions, but not ones we consider when accepting the consolations for grief.

Another concept, but one I haven't heard as much about, is the concept of heaven being a place of eternal rest. This apparently grew out of the age of serfdom when serfs worked long, hard days, six days a week. Sunday, sometimes referred to as the Sabbath, was given to the serfs as a day of rest. I have also heard this used in connection with slaves and slavery in one of the darker periods of American history. Rest was good, and eternal rest would be better. Thus was born the idea death would bring eternal rest from the labors of this world, which was considered a desirable goal of eternity. This world was an evil place in which heavy burdens were placed on people. You were freed of this when you reached your eternal rest in heaven. The traditional concepts of heaven I have mentioned all assume a supernatural deity to whom we can relate and one who will take care of us when this life has ended.

In his book *An Introduction to the Philosophy of Religion*, Peter Bertocci makes the case that doubt is the growing edge of faith. It is this doubt that forces us to look for answers in religion. In religion, we seek solace and help from an external supernatural deity. In religion, we seek answers to what lies beyond the death from which none of us can escape. We need to ask if the primary purpose of belief in God is to guarantee our immortality. Why would one bother to believe in God if there is no immortality? This question is posed in the book *Who is Jesus,* by Crossan & Watts. This takes us back again to the majority of Christians in the survey who said they are Christian to get to heaven. What if there is no heaven? When you remove rewards and

THE HEREAFTER: HEAVEN, HELL, PURGATORY OR...?

punishments from discussions about life after death, most people have not much left to say. The goal of using religion as a tool to prepare us for eternity is entirely missing the point. The goal of religion should be to teach us to live in the here and now in a way that brings the Kingdom of Heaven a little closer to life on Earth. After all, we are already living the life of the ages (eternal life). Eternal life is not something that begins at death, but rather something that begins at birth or, depending on your perspective, before birth.

There are some other points to consider when looking at life after death. First of all, I don't believe there is a separate set of rules that govern life on Earth. Laws controlling life on Earth are laws that govern life in the entire universe. We most likely do not know what all those laws are. I have already referred to theories telling us all matter is connected. That does not prove we descended from the apes, but it is telling us we are linked to them—as well as to potatoes, cabbage, and any other living vegetable or animal life. You see, we now know a common DNA resides in all living things! You don't like broccoli? Regardless, you are connected to it.

I am not a physicist. I do know new theories and research reveal some interesting things. In the growing field of quantum physics, we are now told quantified packages of energy can spontaneously transform into physical waves of measureable energy. Energy is never lost, but can be transformed from one substance to another. An example of this is fire. The combustible material is transformed to heat, gases, and ash residue, but nothing is actually lost, just transformed. Is it possible that at the point of death we are not lost, but transformed into another form of energy? I have already mentioned that the string theory suggests there might be many different dimensions to the universe. Is it possible, at the point of death, the energy form of life in this dimension is transferred into a different energy form in an entirely different dimension? What a range of possibilities are opened by the very idea.

Research is constantly being conducted to try and determine if the mind is more than the brain, or if the mind and brain are one and the same. So far, scientists have only been able to speculate; they have not been able to prove the brain is the mind. Is it possible the mind is an energy that resides somewhere out there—possibly in one of those other dimensions alluded to in string theory? If the mind actually occupies an "out there" dimension, is it also possible somewhere out there is a field of consciousness in which we are all connected? I referred to this in the last chapter and include it again here. If there are different layers or dimensions to our universe and if in some way we are connected together in a field, is it possible in some way we enter a new dimension at the time of death? Is it possible we experience this connectedness in a whole new different way? Carl Jung, born in Switzerland in 1875, spoke of a collective unconscious. Was this man, years before quantum physics and string theory, in his own way sensing in some way we are all connected? You decide.

A phenomenon often referred to as proof of life after death—some would say proof of heaven—is the near-death experience (NDE). Any discussion of life after death would be remiss without touching on the subject of NDE. Major attention was focused on this phenomenon with the publication in 1975 of *Life After Life*, a book by Raymond Moody that went on to become a best seller. Although this book brought the subject to public attention, it was not the beginning of the phenomenon. Experiences similar to NDE can be found in some religious writings, in the writings of Chinese culture, and other ancient writings. An NDE can be described as momentary contact with a completely different type of reality, often described as a brief contact with the other side—the other side being the side beyond death. It is estimated about 20 percent of the people experiencing an NDE give very similar descriptions of the event. NDEs most often occur in situations where the participant is dying or may already have been pronounced dead. There is a sense of leaving the body and being above the scene taking place. One's own body is seen and conversations among those present are heard. Being in a tunnel is a common experience, very often headed toward a very brilliant light. A sense of awe is described as being in the presence of a higher power. This higher power is sometimes described as Jesus, or maybe God. It is not unusual for the individual to hear the voices of relatives or to even see them—often beckoning the individual to join them. A recent book about one person's experience with an NDE is *Proof of Heaven*, by Eben Alexander, M.D., a highly trained neurosurgeon. His story is very convincing about what might exist beyond the grave. In his thinking the "might exist" should be labeled "does exist." He certainly experienced another dimension while declared brain dead for seven days.

We can make several observations about NDEs. Not all experiences are exactly the same. What is seen and heard seems to be a direct reflection of that person's culture and belief system. That simply means, for example, a Christian would not sense the higher power to be Mohammed. If it is true that those from different cultures see and experience NDEs in a way that relates to their culture, it raises an interesting question. Is it possible that in some way we create our own afterlife? Those who doubt the existence of an afterlife claim the experience is simply a trick of the mind—a mental projection. I believe Dr. Eben Alexander would dispute calling it a trick of the mind. I refer back to my discussion about the eleven dimensions related to quantum physics and the string theory—is it possible that an NDE is actually entering into one of these dimensions? I leave that for you to ponder.

A common byproduct of an NDE is a change in the way the person looks at life and death. Very often the result is a stronger belief in the afterlife, showing more compassion to others, and more interest in the spiritual aspects of living. If there was a fear of death before the event, the fear appears to diminish or even disappear. Another byproduct is often less interest in things material.

Not everyone believes an NDE gives a glimpse of what heaven will be like. To some the light especially is suspect. I quote from a book mentioned earlier, *To Hell and Back*, "…it is crucial in near-death studies to determine the source of this being of light—whether the source is a reliable representative of God, or a luring mirage of evil that imitates God as a forgiving Force." This author claims there are as many negative NDEs as positive ones, but they just aren't reported, or, reference the quote above, they read the light wrong. He goes on to claim there are those who relate they have encountered demons or evil forces while trying to make their way to the light. This he explains as part of the continuing battle between good and evil to claim a soul, even to the very end. As this chapter is dealing with the hereafter, we can say that even seeing demons during an NDE could be an indicator of life after death. We could further surmise that the author of the book I quoted would believe for some life after death would be hell—literally!

Another phenomenon less well known is after-death communication (ADC). This is sometimes listed under the category of paranormal activity, but I will treat ADC separately. The term is believed to have been first used by William and Judy Guggenheim, who published a book in 1996, *Hello from Heaven*. The book dealt with ADC experienced by people in mourning over the loss of a person near and dear to them. These experiences are probably more common than most of us realize. This is in part because people who have experienced an ADC are hesitant to talk about it. If you have ever experienced weird stares because of something you said, you know what I mean. An ADC is a contact experienced by a live person from someone who is deceased. How readily would you be to admit it if it happened to you? Keep in mind this is something spontaneous and not brought about by having contacted a psychic, medium, or some such type of interventionist. They occur in a number of different ways, from actually hearing a voice, to just sensing a presence. It is not unusual to have such contact occurring in a dream.

Are ADCs real or imagined? Discounting such contacts when reading about them or listening to someone who relates such an experience is one thing. We all have to make our own judgments as to whether it's real, the figment of imagination, or dire stress. It is another one of those things where I claim to be agnostic. I am not willing to discount the experiences of those who have experienced an ADC. Those who experience them would also say it is another proof there is a continued existence after death. Is it possible the appearances of Jesus to those who saw him after his death could be attributed to the phenomenon of ADC?

THE HEREAFTER: HEAVEN, HELL, PURGATORY OR...?

There are other paranormal activities and psychic phenomena some say prove there is life after death. Who doesn't like a good ghost story? There are many of them available. Many are fiction and have played big in some television series. There are also a sizeable number not considered fiction. There are stories of strange happenings, ghosts haunting certain locations, such as the place a person died years before. These are different than an ADC in that an ADC generally only happens to a close friend or relative. A ghost can appear to anyone. In most cases the ghost seen is of the person who died, often a tragic death, and the spirit of the departed is still troubled and appears from time to time. The appearances of such apparitions are given as proof there is some kind of existence after death. Those who claim to have experienced a sighting of a ghost will not be convinced otherwise. Remember, a person's perception is that person's reality. It is impossible to prove ghosts beyond a doubt. It is also impossible to prove they don't exist beyond any doubt. You decide.

Angel stories generally have a religious flavor to them. The Bible is often quoted as proof there are angels. I suppose if you read the Bible as literal, inerrant history, you could make that case. That view holds no proof for me. I have read accounts and talked with people who swear they have encountered an angel. Their stories say they were protected by a guardian angel, or experienced one in some other way. For some, the encounter was an actual visual encounter. As I have said before, I am not out to prove they did not experience an angel. It is very difficult to disprove what someone says they have experienced. Keep in mind a person's perception is that person's reality. We also need to realize angel terminology is often used to describe the form of one who has passed on from this life. How often have you heard when a child has died words to the effect, "God wanted another angel," or "She's now an angel in heaven"? Maybe so, but again it's one of those things that can't be proven. It might be more accurate to say it can't be proven unless you accept a person's perception of encountering an angel as proof. And to be perfectly honest, neither can it be disproven that angels exist. You decide.

GOD IN A BOX

The last category I will discuss is contact with the dead. This is to be differentiated from anything previously stated, more specifically ADC. I am referring to contact generally initiated and brought about by a third party. There is no lack of psychics who will promise you they can contact a deceased person for you. I would like to have just a fraction of the money spent on charlatans who make such a promise. It would also be wrong for me to say all are charlatans. It is like so much else we have already discussed. There are those who swear they have experienced it and those who swear it can't happen. It might be of interest to note this is not a new phenomenon.

For those who like a biblical reference for everything, we can provide one here. Based on how I read scripture, I don't take this story as literal or factual. It is an interesting story, or should I say an interesting religious myth? In 1 Samuel, the story is told of Saul contacting a medium, often referred to as the Witch of Endor. An interesting aspect of this story is how Saul had expelled the mediums and the wizards. Now he was fearful of the Philistines and wanted to consult with Samuel, who was dead. Saul chose to do this through a medium. The medium was able to contact Samuel. Samuel was not happy about it. Saul made known his problem, and Samuel's answer was not what Saul wanted to hear. Jumping to the end of the story, what Samuel said would happen did happen. If you want to know more, read the story. You can find it in 1 Samuel 28:3-19. The point here is not to dissect the story, but to point out that contacting someone who is dead through use of a third party is not a new phenomenon.

The term "crossing over" is sometimes used to describe contacting a deceased person. *Crossing Over* is the title of a book by John Edward. There was also a television show, *Crossing Over with John Edward*. On October 5, 1999, he was the subject of a ninety-minute HBO special, *Life After Life*. He is not the only psychic medium who claims to have contact with those on the other side of life, but he is certainly one of the best known. Can mediums do what they claim? It's difficult to prove beyond a doubt they can, and it's difficult to prove beyond a doubt they can't. I chose John Edward because I have read some of his

THE HEREAFTER: HEAVEN, HELL, PURGATORY OR...?

work and some of the criticisms of his work. I have watched a few of his television programs. I also chose him because of attendance at a John Edward public program and having watched him at work.

In 2004, my wife and I were driving across Canada on our way to Alaska, staying in campgrounds en route. One of our stops was in Edmonton, British Columbia, Canada. A brochure in the campground office advertised that John Edward was appearing in Edmonton during our stay. Having read some of his work and being very curious about his claims, we decided to go. The event was held in a large auditorium and it was full. It turned out to be an interesting evening. He started slowly warming up the crowd and talking some about the things he did. Gradually, he moved into what he does and began receiving messages from the other side and pointing to different sections of the audience. The person trying to be contacted was supposedly in the area of the audience where he pointed. He would give first letters of names, sometimes names, and sometimes cause of death or other pieces of information about the person trying to make contact. Several people seemed to make successful contact with someone from the other side.

As he moved through the audience, he kept getting closer to where we were sitting. He said he was getting a message for someone in our area. A few people in the general area spoke up. After Edward asked a few questions, he would say they were not who the person on the other side was trying to contact. He pointed almost right at us and said he thought the message was for someone in our area. The lady beside me got very excited and thought the message might be for her. The cause of death and the first letter of the name fit one of her relatives. She stood up and was questioned, a little more than previous volunteers because Edwards thought the message was particularly strong for someone in our area. After a number of questions, he determined she was not the person trying to be contacted.

He stayed with our area for a while longer. He kept saying the message was strong for someone in our area. He said it was a female trying to make contact and he thought her first name started with an "L." He also said he was getting information she had died of some disease, possibly leukemia, or at least some type of blood disease. He finally gave up making the contact he thought was there. Soon after, the program ended.

My wife and I were discussing all we had observed as we drove back to the campground. We were trying to determine if what we had seen was real or some kind of a rigged performance. If it was rigged, we decided it was well done. Our conversation lagged and we were driving in silence. Suddenly my wife spoke up. "Lois died of a blood disease!" Lois was her sister and she had died of a blood disease a few years before. That never occurred to either of us. Did my wife miss an opportunity to receive a contact from her sister on the other side? We will never know the answer to that question. What we do know is it raised more questions than answers on whether or not those who have died can make contact with the living. What we experienced was more believable than the healings I saw take place at an Oral Roberts' healing service many years before.

After all I have written, am I any closer to an answer proving beyond doubt the existence of a hereafter? I rather doubt it. What some would see as proof, others would see as pure speculation. Some of what I have written would seem to indicate there is something out there beyond this life. Some like to call it heaven, some like to call it hell, and even purgatory gets thrown into the mix. I don't like any of those terms. Whatever is out there I like to think it starts here, on this side of the hereafter. About the hereafter, we can only speculate. If you live fully, lovingly, and show compassion here, you don't need to be concerned about the after. I base this in large part on words of Paul in Romans 8:38, *"For I am convinced that neither death, nor life, nor angels, nor rulers, nor things present, nor things to come, nor powers, nor height, nor depth, nor anything else in all creation, will be able to separate us from the love of God in Christ Jesus our Lord."* A life lived to the highest capability of an individual, showing love and compassion, would follow along the guidelines set by St. Augustine when he said words to the effect, "Love God and do as you please."

I know there are those who will say you better be concerned about

THE HEREAFTER: HEAVEN, HELL, PURGATORY OR...?

the here because it determines the after. Those kinds of statements come from people who have a heaven/hell view of the hereafter. You better be saved here, or it will be rough after. Saved from what and to what? If you ask that question, the answer will often be something like, "Saved from hell and saved to heaven." That takes us back to the study I quoted which said a majority of people surveyed said they were Christian to make sure they got to heaven. I don't believe heaven and hell are what the game is about. Perhaps they have forgotten the meaning of grace. To me, it means no requirement for salvation. Proclaiming that you need to be a confessing Christian could be construed as a requirement. Even the word salvation requires a new look. Marcus J. Borg, in his book *Speaking Christian*, equates the modern usage of the term salvation with getting to heaven. He points out that the word appears numerous times in the Old Testament. At that time there was no concept of an afterlife as we define it. He pointed out its more relevant meaning was freedom from bondage. I like that as there can be many things to which one can be in bondage. Getting rid of the bondage baggage can be a very freeing experience. This baggage could also include the "correct beliefs" one must hold in order to obtain salvation (present day definition) or to be saved.

We can probably agree the hereafter is eternity. Maybe if you believe in reincarnation, you would disagree with that statement. If reincarnation happens, it probably goes on for an eternity. It is difficult to conceive of eternity because it is infinite and we are finite. How can you describe something you have never experienced? On the other hand, maybe we are experiencing eternity in the present. The gospel of John certainly gives credibility to such thinking. It could be said the great hope of the gospel of John is about eternal life, sometimes referred to as the life of the ages. John 6:47 quotes Jesus as saying, *"Very truly, I tell you, whoever believes has eternal life."* Those words are not written in a future tense but in a present tense. At the raising of Lazarus, John quotes Jesus as saying, *"...and everyone who lives and believes in me will never die"* (John 11:26). Those are rather strong words. You might be ready to call me on that because I said earlier that everyone dies. It depends on what you mean by death. The body does die, and Jesus is probably referring to something about us which doesn't die. Is it possible that eternity is something found as we go deeper into ourselves? Is it possible that eternity is within us? One thing I don't find in the New Testament is a lot of time spent by Jesus trying to make his followers believers in immortality. Through his words and actions, he spent a great amount of time introducing his followers into a quality of life never before seen in a human being. This was a quality of life that he wanted them to also experience. It was a life freed of "shoulds" and "oughts." It was a life lived in service to others, not lived to dominate others. It was a life showing compassion to others, not judgment of others.

Whatever else we want to do about the hereafter, we need to at least get rid of the heaven and hell mentality. To me, heaven and hell are not what it is all about. It is about how we live here. Eternity is already inside the soul of humans. How we live here probably does have implications on our hereafter, but not in the sense that decisions about God can only be made before we die. This is in contradiction to fundamentalist belief. Being saved is important to the fundamentalist mindset, and they believe it must happen before one dies as there are no second chances. I have even heard great rejoicing over deathbed confessions. Deathbed confessions mean nothing to me. The grace of God is present and available, deathbed confession or no deathbed confession. We very much limit the love and grace of God when we confine receiving it to only the physical lifetime in a live body. In *Life After Death*, Deepak Chopra states, "We are mind and spirit first, and that places our home beyond the stars." It is this mind and spirit for whom God is always present and for whom God's grace is always available—this life or the next.

My thoughts need not be your thoughts, but I will break my thoughts down to a few sentences. The hereafter, or eternity if you prefer, is another dimension of a universe filled with many dimensions, some not yet fully understood. The spirit, or soul if you prefer, may already be in that dimension. We prepare for how we do our dying by

THE HEREAFTER: HEAVEN, HELL, PURGATORY OR...?

how we do our living. Life after death should be seen as a progression, not a destination. I like the words of Harry Emerson Fosdick in his book *A Guide to Understanding the Bible*, when he says, "...death is an open door through which the soul's life with God moves on."

One last thing for you to ponder. Is it possible for NDEs, ADCs, ghost stories, angel sightings, and contact with the dead to be manifestations of a connectedness existing between both living and dead? Is it possible this is a connectedness that takes place in one of those eleven dimensions not yet seen? Is there an afterlife? You decide.

7

RELIGION: HOW? WHY?

Religion is sometimes defined as the service to and worship of God or the supernatural. It can also be defined as a system of institutionalized religious attitudes, beliefs, and practices by an individual or a group. These are similar to what you might find in a dictionary. I'm sure there are other definitions, but those two will get us on our way. Those words may define religion but are far from answering how and why. To discover an answer to those two questions, we need to look far beyond any dictionary. An academic definition does not explain why individuals choose to be religious. Nor does it explain the impact religion can have on the lives of the followers of a particular religion. In this chapter I will delve into these questions as well as how religion may have come about.

I do believe there is an innate desire in humankind to reach out to a power believed to exist beyond oneself. In Alcoholics Anonymous, it is referred to as a "higher power." Some neurologists now believe there might be a spiritual center in the brain. If so, that might be the trigger for an inner desire to reach out to a power beyond oneself. Note that I said spiritual center in the brain, not religious center. This spiritual center may be one of the reasons why people reach out to religion or become religious—to nourish that spiritual center. Even if this is true, it is not the only way the spiritual center can be nourished. It may,

RELIGION: HOW? WHY?

however, give a clue as to why and how religions came into being.

Like many other things, there is no way to prove the exact beginning of religion. It may very well have been around for at least 30,000 years. Cave art discovered in Europe, estimated to be produced as long as 30,000 years ago, can be interpreted as having religious themes. There is evidence that human fossil remains of this period may have been ritually buried. This is considered further evidence of religious activity. There is speculation that religion started at the same time as humans developed a consciousness of self. Some estimates have dated this development as long as 250,000 years ago, but it could have been much more recent. How did this come about? The ancient humans saw death all around them. They certainly saw it in the animals they ate. They also saw it happen to other members of their tribe or family. Seeing death happen all around them certainly had to have an impact. One day, an ancient human had an insight that was human history changing: "Hey, guess what? We are all going to die someday!" No other animal has this awareness.

Religion may have started in much the same way and maybe in the same timeframe that belief in gods developed. It may have started as a way to influence or appease the gods they had created. It may have been an attempt to explain happenings that could not be explained by the limited knowledge early human beings had at their disposal. An example could be thunder and lightning, which were interpreted to signify the gods were not pleased. Religion was developed to find out what pleased the gods and brought the gods pleasure, rather than displeasure. With the awareness that death was the lot of everyone, religion may also have been a way to give humans an edge on the forces that could cause their demise. Please the gods and they will be on your side.

Another theory states that religion was started by the Cro-Magnons, who have also been credited with starting culture, about 40,000 years ago. This goes further back than the cave art discovered in Europe. Cro-Magnons are considered to be early Homo sapiens.

There are many theories about the origin of religion. What seems to be universally believed is religion came about as a way to placate the gods humans had created. It was also experimental religion. It was not as locked in as some of our religious beliefs are in the present age. If one religious idea didn't appear to work, that was not a problem; simply replace it with a different idea until you found a workable system that placated the gods. I would speculate the process was not quick, but took years for replacement ideas to be put in place. First it would have been concluded the old god wasn't answering the need. Then a new god would have to be encountered who was perceived to meet needs. It would be difficult to determine what happenings would put that process in motion. It may even have been hearing about a neighboring tribe's god and thinking that tribe's god was giving the neighboring tribe better results. It is difficult to imagine how many changes must have been made over the centuries, especially if you believe the gods can be placated. The way in which humankind created their religions is similar to the way in which humankind created their gods. I think it would be safe to say creating gods and creating religions progressed simultaneously.

Another aspect of the lives of the early ancient people addresses the sense of their awareness of the spiritual or holy. According to Rudolf Otto, a German historian of religion, a sense of the "numinous" was basic to religion. This simply means there was a sense that surrounding them were spirits or gods. People believed unknown powers surrounded them in some invisible and unexplainable way. This could be sensed in excitement, calm, dread, awe, and humility as they tried to perceive the mysterious forces they could not explain. Spirits or gods were thought to inhabit places and things and to cause acts of nature. Myths grew up and humans developed rituals of worship to these gods. What is interesting to note is that myths and worship were not developed as an attempt to find literal explanations for that which they did not understand or could not explain. Cave paintings, figurine carvings, myths, and religious ritual were attempts to express their awe and in some way link into the power perceived as belonging to these spirits and mysterious forces. Myths were stories not to be taken literally. They

RELIGION: HOW? WHY?

were seen as symbolic ways to describe complex and mysterious powers, or gods, that words could not explain. These spirits or gods, as they defined them, had characteristics to which humans could aspire. They were also a prototype of human existence. Being able to fashion one's behavior after a god became an important religious idea. You think the idea is absurd? For a present-day example, why is it we rest one day a week, the Sabbath or Sunday?

The presence of spirits was applied to almost every force that could not be understood. Their God boxes probably held more than one god. For example, there were spirits in the forces of nature. What becomes apparent from ancient times to the present is the use of the word "spirit" in the development and tenets of religious thought. It could be used to describe an unknown presence or representing the presence of a god. Those first humans who experienced the reality and frightening concept of self-consciousness were faced with new anxieties. How do you prepare yourself to deal with new anxieties growing out of thoughts concerning isolation, meaning and purpose of life, and most of all one's own ending—or death? They were, without doubt, desperate to find answers. The spirits were the best available candidates to turn to for answers. Maybe turning to the spirits would help them find answers and understand these new life anxieties. They needed to somehow contact a spirit and influence the spirit's power for the benefit of themselves or their tribe. How else could they be protected against the forces of nature when its spirits unleashed its fury against them? Furthermore, if they could influence this spirit, maybe it could be persuaded to come to their aid anytime they were distressed or in danger. Take the discovery of self-consciousness and combine it with an increase in the concept of spirits or gods everywhere and presto, religion is born. Anthropologists tell us this may have been the first recognizable religion of ancient humans, referred to as "animism." This is the idea that god or gods are the invisible forces everywhere and in everything, and not constrained to any one location.

Somewhere along the progression of believing in spirits, the idea developed that each human has a spirit. The convincing experiences that started and kept alive this idea were dreams the ancient people had about friends and family who had died. With no understanding of what dreams were and what caused them, they reached their own conclusions. It must be the spirit, which came to be known as soul, of the deceased. This soul must be continuing to live after death, but invisible to the human eye. The idea developed that these souls had left the body but were still around. This led to a worship of these souls—and to worship of the objects they were thought to inhabit.

It is possible that initially the main purpose of religion was to enlist the help of spirits/gods/souls to be on call. The call would be for protective help against any unknown or calamity that might befall a human being. There were probably stories told about how some spirit or god called upon had provided relief or protection in some manner. Religion provided emotional and spiritual comfort for human beings faced with an enormity of things unknown. We shouldn't jump too quickly to being critical of what might be considered a superstitious belief. In our present day, stories are still told about how a person's god saved that person from harm, disaster, a dreaded disease, or even death. Today some call those instances miracles wrought by a god. Woe unto anyone who would dare to tell the person a god had nothing to do with it.

The concept above was primarily found in the hunter/gatherer societies. As the centuries passed, some human beings became planters/harvesters, and agricultural communities were born. There were still spirits and gods, but they became more precisely defined. The idea of some type of Earth goddess developed. Humans saw plants and living things by which humans were sustained seemingly growing up and being sustained by the Earth. The Earth must be something like a womb. Emphasis shifted to worshipping and satisfying this spirit of Mother Earth's womb. Ergo, the Earth goddess was born. This caused a move away from attaching unknown spirits to everything else around them. The divine was being seen in the feminine, especially in the Earth goddess, who became the feminine symbol of the Earth's womb of fertility. That concept had a lasting impression. Mother Nature and Mother

RELIGION: HOW? WHY?

Earth are feminine concepts in all cultures of the world.

This point in the history of humankind had a decided effect on the history of religion. Since there is an Earth goddess, how do you placate and serve her? Reproduction was what the Earth goddess brought about, so religious rituals should be related in some way. This brought about the glorification of reproduction. Sex became a part of religious ritual in serving the Earth goddess. This Earth goddess religion resulted in both female and male prostitution becoming fixtures in religious worship.

Somewhere along the way, we have the development of tribal religion. The early Israelites' worship of Yahweh would meet the qualifications of a tribal religion. Yahweh was male, as tribal gods were prone to be. The people regularly depended on Yahweh to be their protector, which was an important aspect of a tribal deity. This protection was to be their reward for worshipping the tribal deity. The three-tiered universe puts the heavens above all, and tribal gods were up there somewhere. Out of the heavens came the sun, which provided light and warmth. Also out of the heavens came the rain that nourished and provided sustenance to the land. The mysterious forces of the wind also were perceived to come from the heavens. All these things perceived to be coming from the heavens could be helpful, but also destructive. The tribal deity must be up there causing those things to happen. Good things happened if the tribal god was pleased, and bad things happened if the tribal god wasn't pleased. Tribal deities generally had a chosen people, and certainly the Israelites believed they were Yahweh's chosen people. Polytheism was accepted, and other gods were believed to exist at this time, but only Yahweh was their god and only the Israelites were Yahweh's chosen.

It is no far reach to assume the values of a tribal deity reflected tribal values. I leave it to you to determine who decided those values, the deity or the tribe. There may be something here related to how humans create their own gods who manifest many similarities to humans. You can be sure that if a tribe hated another tribe, the tribal deity would hate that tribe as well. As long as the tribe worshipped and carried

GOD IN A BOX

out the tribal god's perceived commands, all would be well with the tribe, and it could overcome any obstacle. A couple of examples from the Old Testament can be used to illustrate this. Was Egypt's Pharaoh able to withstand the onslaught of plagues sent by the Israelites' deity, Yahweh? What chance did the Amorites have against Joshua when the tribal god Yahweh caused the sun to stand still so Joshua could see to kill more of the enemy? You can read the entire story in Joshua 10. Especially supportive of a tribal god supporting the tribe is in verse 14. *"There has been no day like it before or since, when the Lord heeded a human voice; for the Lord fought for Israel."*

Many times when tribes were at war, the defeated tribe's god disappeared from the scene and the god of the conquering tribe was accepted. The Jewish tribes of the northern kingdom did intermarry with their conquerors and also accepted their gods. They disappeared from history. The Jewish tribes of the southern kingdom were more adept at keeping the tribal god Yahweh when they were conquered. They were not completely immune, and at times would accept some things about other tribal deities. This is what sometimes caused them trouble with Yahweh. They kept their identity and did not disappear from history.

When we read some of the prophets of the Old Testament, another step in the development of religion is present. We see the prophetic role as transforming the concept of tribal deity into a much more inclusive god. Polytheism was still a part of the world of belief, but the prophets were intent on showing Yahweh as the only true God, and all other gods were false. The prophets also were intent on showing Yahweh as more than just a masculine figure who made his home in the heavens. Some of the prophets saw Yahweh (God) defined by certain attributes. The story Hosea told revealed a God of love. Amos described God as justice, and the Israelite (Jewish) people were adamant that justice be served. We may need to focus on Micah again in the twenty-first century. He wanted people to realize that God's demands were more focused on how they lived than on how they worshipped. In one last illustration, Malachi puts a cap on it all by proclaiming God as a universal presence or *"great among the nations"* (Mal. 1:11).

RELIGION: HOW? WHY?

It might be of interest to note that during this progression in the development of religion, the feminine aspects associated with gods and worship became less important and in many ways faded from sight. Some feminine aspects did not disappear completely and are still present today, albeit in a little different way. The veneration of the Virgin Mary in Christendom is certainly feminine. The church is referred to as "she" and never "he." Mother Church is also a common term still in use.

There are many religions in the world today. Of these, there are three main groups I will mention. At least two of them had tribal beginnings. Using the term "tribal" may be confusing and too broad, but I think it will help bring home the concept. It may be more accurate to describe them as regional religions. We who are part of the Western world experience a predominance of the Judeo-Christian God portrayed in the Old Testament and the New Testament. The God of the people of Israel would certainly be considered tribal in the beginning. As Christianity grew out of Judaism, its heritage would be related to Jewish heritage.

Are you more aware of Middle Eastern countries since the destruction of the World Trade Center towers on 9/11? Our world has grown smaller, and communication media has broadened our knowledge base. If you visit a Middle Eastern country, you will be confronted with Muslims and their belief in Allah and the Koran. Islam can be traced to tribal beginnings. In the Far East, we have the birthplace of the eastern religions. There are many variations of eastern religions. The most familiar to most people are Hindu and Buddhist practices. Both Middle Eastern and Far Eastern religions are making inroads into the Western world. This is a very scary to some followers of Western religions. Possibly one of the reasons more people are taking up the practice of Middle Eastern and Far Eastern religions in the Western world could be related to disillusionment with the Judeo-Christian Western world religion.

We find ourselves already over a decade into the twenty-first century of the Common Era. How many centuries Before the Common Era did human beings determine the gods caused wind, fire, lightning, and thunder, or any other force of nature that left them fearful? How many centuries Before the Common Era did human beings decide these gods must be placated and establish some form of ritual that would garner their favor? It was certainly better to have these gods on your side than against you. How did humans determine what worked and what didn't? They developed rituals and experimented to find those practices that would help relieve human anxieties. It is impossible to answer how they chose what they did, but somewhere along the way, someone decided what worked and what didn't. Was the decision based on actual proof by experimenting and choosing one ritual that seemed to work better than another? This was probably not how it worked. There may have been more coincidence than fact involved in the choosing. Maybe some rituals were chosen because a powerful charismatic leader said that was the way it was going to be. Charismatic leaders can have a powerful influence on what happens. Leader choices are not always based on facts. Sometimes they are based on personal likes or bias. Maybe it was just a strong political leader who dictated the guidelines. Did Constantine have any influence over the Council of Nicea? It took place in 325 A.D. and was ordered to happen by the Roman Emperor Caesar Flavius Constantine. Emperor Constantine himself presided over a meeting of church bishops and leaders. The declared purpose was to define the true God for all of Christianity and for all time. Out of this council came the Nicene Creed—still in use today!

Another very important thought to keep in mind is since humans created their gods, it would give them good insight into what would be pleasing to their gods. One thing certain is that once in place, rituals and practices became law, and to change them was almost impossible. (Once those rituals are placed in the God box, you better not mess with them.) It didn't make any difference if in later years it was determined the rituals and practices didn't change anything. The rituals and practices remained unchangeable. A good example would be the Nicene Creed, which is still used in many churches today. The Nicene Creed was written in the fourth century! I talk to many people who say

RELIGION: HOW? WHY?

they don't believe in it literally anymore. They ask why we don't make a change. Have you ever heard the phrase "But we have always done it this way"? I add to that, "And we will keep on doing it this way even if it doesn't work!" After all, the Nicene Creed was to settle the issue for all time. Is literal belief in the Nicene Creed in your God box?

Jump now into the twenty-first century, more particularly the Western world. What has really changed? In my opinion, very little. With the diminished belief in powerful feminine gods, gods were considered to be male. What gender is most often applied to the God of the Western world? There seems to be little doubt the perception is of a male God. In primitive religions, the gods were somewhere out there, or external. Where is the God of the Western world located? For many people, God is somewhere out there in the heavens, or external. In primitive religions, the gods had supernatural powers. It was important to appease the gods so they would use their supernatural powers to come to the aid of a human in need or in danger. Is that much different from the Christian God of the twenty-first century Western world? The most revered God of the Western world must also be appeased in order to gain assistance, favor, and protection. Somewhere along the way, hope for appeasement was added to guarantee eternal life in heaven in the hereafter.

There is an important similar aspect in the minds of both primitive humans and modern humans concerning what needs to be done to appease this male deity residing somewhere out there. What needed to be done was what comprised religious rituals and practices in primitive religions. Is it not the same concept comprising rituals and practices of present-day religions? The rituals and practices were designed to keep the gods appeased and also to meet human needs. They became religions—religions that were not divinely inspired, but designed by humans to gain favor with the gods. Religion fulfilled the human need to believe they had earned the favor of the gods and were deserving of divine protection. And the gods expected to be worshipped. They expected humans to consider themselves unworthy in their sight. Maybe you should consider whether or not this is what humans thought the gods wanted. Did the gods ever speak to tell humans why and how to worship? I know there are plenty of people out there who will say, "God told me…" Did God really tell the person, or is it the person's assumption of what God wants? Draw your own conclusions.

Several conclusions can be reached from this. The one that seems most logical to me is that humankind created their religions to appease their created gods. The subtlety of this is how the created religion becomes a human attempt at manipulation of their created god. Religious rituals and practices are often no more than attempts to influence their god. Why do we gather in praise and worship? Why do we confess our sins, call ourselves "miserable sinners," and proclaim our unworthiness? Is all this nothing more than an attempt to influence an external, all-powerful, supernatural deity by building up brownie points? But for what purpose do we need brownie points? We live with the assumption that when we have needs, when we are in trouble or danger, we can cash in the brownie points for divine help and protection. Religious worship becomes an overt act of flattery by which we hope to put an obligation on the supernatural deity to respond to our requests. That shifts into high gear when we contemplate dying and eternity.

Because I am a Christian and know more about the Christian religion than any other religion, that's where my focus lies. Remember the majority who are Christian to make sure they get to heaven? We need to keep the Christian God happy, and proclaiming to be a Christian, confessing, and worshipping may get you the brownie points you need to make it. We use the term "Lord have mercy" in worship, almost like a serf cowering in fear of the king. This gives an indication of how some view God and might also be their prayer as they face eternity—for those who think it means standing in fear and trembling.

Religion doesn't stop at just rituals and worship. There are numerous rules of God that must be followed. These rules have been written down by humans who knew exactly what God said those rules were to be. Again, it needs to be pointed out that they know because they are the same humans who created God, and thus know his rules. You please the deity by keeping these rules. Almost everyone is familiar

RELIGION: HOW? WHY?

with the song "Santa Claus Is Coming to Town." Some of the lines in that song keep children from doing anything out of order, especially around Christmas. "He sees you when you're sleeping, he knows when you're awake; he knows when you've been bad or good, so be good for goodness sake!" Now doesn't that have a familiar ring to it? I don't how many times I have heard of the Book of Life in which all your deeds are written down. You will be judged and answer to them at the judgment day in eternity. When the Book of Life is opened, will you be listed? To enlighten you, the Book of Life (Revelation 20:11-15) is the book believed by some to contain the names of all those who have been "born again" or "saved." They believe this book contains the names of those who will live in heaven forever with God. This is not a belief you will find in my God box! It appears to me for many people God is nothing more than a celestial Santa Claus—or maybe I should say a celestial judge. Maybe celestial bookkeeper would be even more accurate. Keep the rules, because he is watching you! Santa Claus is coming to town, Jesus is coming back, God is watching you, and some day the Book of Life will be opened!

Comedian George Carlin was raised in the Roman Catholic faith, but as an adult never practiced it. Religion, God, and particularly religious adherents were frequent subjects of criticism in his routines. Even though scathing in his criticisms of religion, he often hit on issues that existed, even if it angered religious adherents. In one of his routines, he talks about an invisible man who lives in the sky and is watching everything you do, with a list of ten things you better not do. Carlin then says, "And if you do any of these things, he will send you to a special place of burning and fire and smoke and torture and anguish for you to live forever, and suffer, and suffer, and burn, and scream, until the end of time. But he loves you. He loves you. He loves you and he needs money."

You don't think religion has any control over human behavior? Think again! Throughout the past 2,000 years, the Christian church has established a rather elaborate structure. This structure includes hierarchy, doctrine, dogma, creeds, and rituals. There can be a lot of variations among denominations, but a structure of some type exists in all of them. Even those who claim to have no formal structure, rituals, creeds, or dogma have an informal one. In their own way, the informal structures can be as unbending and rigid as the formal structures. Sometimes I think they are more powerful than the formal ones, simply because they give more leeway for interpretation. There is no established hierarchy or written creed to use as an authority, so individuals become the authority. People have been executed for disagreeing with those in control of established religious belief. Ever hear of the Inquisition or the Salem witch trials? People have been tortured until they confessed to "correct beliefs" and then executed before they change their mind. People have been ostracized for disagreeing. I mentioned Galileo earlier in this book. He was one who was placed under what was basically house arrest for the last years of his life. His discoveries dared to challenge the stated and accepted beliefs of the religious hierarchy.

Karl Marx proclaimed that religion was the opiate of the people. He was aware of how the church he experienced controlled the lives of its adherents. It was like giving them opium, keeping them drugged and under control. There can be no doubt in a study of history that there is a dark side of all religions that reveals abuse of power and control. Control is still present in our generation. There are still mortal sins that will keep you out of heaven. That is a control issue because the church can provide you forgiveness and you can still get in, if you keep the rules.

Earlier in this book I talked about the fundamentalist mindset and their emphasis on the importance of "correct beliefs." One of those beliefs centers around the Bible to be literally and factually true. Their truth depends on historical authenticity. There is a great control issue here. Questioning one iota puts you on a slippery slope, headed for eternal damnation. Believe in Jesus or go to hell. Christianity is the only way to salvation. I think one definition of fundamentalist faith (in any denomination or faith group) could be to believe in things that don't always make sense. Remember, Caleb was taught 2 + 2 = 3.

RELIGION: HOW? WHY?

It is not difficult to encounter those who say they need not be religious. They may even point to the dark side of the history of the Christian church and say they don't need to be a part of an institution with such a past. It is not my intent to have what I have said about religion used for such a purpose. There is the positive side of religion, and it must also be recognized. It is not necessary to go into a lot of detail, because you will either believe religion has a good side or believe it doesn't.

The America in which we live came about because people were seeking a place where they could have freedom of expression for their religious faith. The Constitution of the United States was founded on basically Judeo-Christian principles. Some of the great institutions of higher learning in the United States were started as places to train clergy. Hospitals came about because of concerns of religious people. Many of the social movements for the betterment of our nation had religious leaders at the forefront. Charity has always been a prime concern of religious people. Religious people contribute more time, money, and resources to assist the needs of others than do non-religious people. Walter Rauschenbusch, often called the father of the social gospel, said the true test of any theology is its social effects. I change theology to religion and say the true test of religion is its social effect. I would apply the same test to those who say they are spiritual and not religious. Does one's religion or spirituality make any difference in that person's life? Does it have any effect on how one views one's neighbors? Does it make any difference in how one responds to needs of others? If it doesn't make a difference that includes compassion, concern, and action, I would declare the religiosity or spirituality as nothing more than a facade—a facade that presents to the world an image that is not indicative of the person's true motivation and identity. Religion for me speaks of community. It is in community that compassion can have its strongest outpouring on those in need. It is in a committed religious community where to be committed means to be active. Being spiritual but not religious speaks to me of being a loner. Being a loner requires no commitment and no action.

GOD IN A BOX

I have heard people say religion is just a crutch, and religion is only for weak people who are unable to stand on their own. My reply is, what's wrong with a crutch if it helps you walk better? Have you ever taken an aspirin for an ache or pain? Have you ever used some type of healing ointment on a wound? Have you ever received an antibiotic for an infection? Have you received immunization inoculations for any type of disease? Have you ever received a flu vaccine? Do you wear glasses, contact lenses, or hearing aids? Aren't these things also a type of crutch? Are these only for weak people who can't heal or fight disease on their own?

Some say religion is just for women and children. It is true; many churches have more female attendees than male. Church is not considered masculine enough for macho men. There is an impression that equates being religious to being a weakling or effeminate. I'm not sure where or how that concept got started. Maybe we need more macho Jesus pictures.

Look at the lives of Jesus, Paul, the apostles. Look at some of the great saints of the church. How about St. Francis of Assisi? Moving closer to our age, you might want to look at John Calvin, Martin Luther, and John Knox. Certainly we need to consider John Wesley. Even closer, take a look at Dietrich Bonhoeffer. He was a German pastor who left the safety of the United States and returned to his native Germany. He publicly repudiated the Nazis and opposed Hitler's persecution of the Jews. He was involved in a failed plot to assassinate Hitler and was arrested and hanged. More recently, look at the life of Dr. Martin Luther King. Tell me what was weak about any of those men? If you don't know anything about them, I suggest you look them up and do some catch-up reading.

Active membership with a church can provide opportunity for fellowship, for education, for support, and for service. I really emphasize the fellowship aspect. You can be spiritual by yourself, but religion provides an opportunity to put that spirituality to work in an organized manner. I believe it can also nurture the spiritual. These are things you will find in my God box.

RELIGION: HOW? WHY?

If you are spiritual and not connected to others, how is your spirituality used in reaching out to those who have needs? A church can provide a sense of community, including a healthy atmosphere of support. A church can provide opportunities to be of service to those in need. Classes and worship services need not be boring experiences. They can be vibrant, alive, and opportunities for learning. Notice I said *active* membership. It is my firm belief that if you aren't active, you will be more likely to believe religion has no value and you will become a dropout. There are people of all ages who voice the claim they find religion less than satisfying. Level of satisfaction is closely related to level of involvement. Returns on almost anything are directly related to what is invested. You get out of something what you put into it. Not satisfied? What do you have invested?

I realize I am on shaky ground when I say to get active in a church, especially when I can be critical of religion. Picking the right church is of the utmost importance. One denomination proclaims "open doors, open hearts, open minds." That to me would certainly be a requirement. I would certainly want it to be a church whose emphasis is on practicing the teachings of Jesus rather than just an emphasis on believing the correct things about Jesus. A mind belief does not always lead to an accepting, forgiving, loving, and serving attitude. Sometimes the exact opposite can occur. A person with a mindset of "correct beliefs" can be judgmental and hostile. Persons with that mindset may not be accepting of anyone who does not see eye to eye with their beliefs. You may have to look, but there are churches more concerned with you as an individual than as someone to convert. There are churches more concerned with the transformation in your life by helping you to live as Jesus lived, rather than whether you walk down the aisle and proclaim "I believe!"

A few paragraphs back I referred to those who are spiritual, but not religious. That word can be used about a new category of believers in our age. These are individuals who consider themselves to be spiritual but not religious, abbreviated as SBNR. Is that actually possible? As I have stated earlier, I believe everyone has a spiritual nature, even if some do not recognize it. So yes, it is possible to be spiritual but not religious. What does the spiritual but not religious person do? I suppose they commune with God in some way, practice some kind of meditation or prayer, but I really can't answer for them. Some have been turned off by organized religion in childhood, by some incident in a church to which they once belonged, or some other perception, whether founded on facts or not. Of no small matter has been the issue of sexual molestation in the Roman Catholic Church.

In some way they have been disillusioned by the message they hear from organized religion. This I know: Whatever their perception, it is their reality. What is their answer? For some the answer is nominal religiosity and for others it is no religiosity. Some just don't want to make a commitment. That is certainly nothing new in our present age. Many organizations are having trouble keeping membership roles filled. We may be living in an age of "non-joiners," whatever the organization may be.

Maybe their criticism of religion, Christianity in particular, is based on what they understand Christianity should be, contrasted with what they see practiced by Christians. They question whether Christianity is about love, acceptance, forgiveness, and practicing what Jesus taught, or is it about subscribing to a particular set of "correct beliefs"? They have a longing for things spiritual, but for whatever the reason, church does not meet their needs in this dimension. Some don't want to admit a connection to any religious organization. Neither do they want to be seen as not believing in God or a higher power—whatever that higher power may be. They solve the dilemma by just calling themselves "spiritual." Being spiritual sounds sort of religious but escapes all the trappings and dogma they envision goes with religion. Being spiritual but not religious insulates from having to commit time or money to an organization. It also gives freedom to hold a wide range of beliefs not locked into any particular creed.

The "none" group also needs to be mentioned. This group has grown considerably in recent years. They are the ones who when asked about religious preference answer "none." This comprises a group that I

RELIGION: HOW? WHY?

would label as religiously illiterate. They were not raised in the church, and may know very little about religion. Or, what they have heard about religion was negative and they make an effort to avoid it. They may have heard something about everyone having a spirit. If questioned about religion an easy answer is spiritual but not religious.

There is another issue I believe may be lurking in the shadows. Maybe those who are spiritual but not religious still hold to a shadow belief there is "a man upstairs." By claiming to be spiritual, they are keeping that door open and the bases covered. Sometime in the future there may still be a need to have something or someone "up there" in a security-producing role. The supernatural theistic deity is dying. As it dies, it may appear that organized religion may be dying also. Claiming to be spiritual but not religious could be an attempt to let go and hang on at the same time. Let go of the supernatural theist deity, but hang on to something—just in case!

What about the other side—can a person be religious and not be spiritual? Based on what I have said earlier, I don't see how it would be possible for a person to be religious but not spiritual. I have said everyone has a spiritual dimension. It may be possible a religious person is not in touch with the spiritual dimension or may not be using it in an effective manner. I believe the spiritual dimension is a good dimension of a human being and drives compassionate behavior. I believe Dr. Alexander, in *Proof of Heaven*, would support that concept. He states, "How do we get closer to this genuine spiritual self? By manifesting love and compassion. Why? ...They are real. They are concrete. And they make up the very fabric of the spiritual realm." It could be possible for the spiritual dimension to be so deeply submerged beneath hateful things that it becomes hard to get in touch with it. It might be possible in such a situation for a person to look religious—following the rules, but not look spiritual—showing love and compassion. This ends up being one of those questions for which I have no answer. It is one of those questions needing to be answered personally by each individual.

Whether religious, spiritual, or both is something that must be determined by each person individually. What is your attitude toward religion? In religion, many people are seeking security and not truth. Whatever your views toward organized religion, are you willing to ask serious questions about your attitude toward religion? If so, there are several questions I deem to be important. It is time to again look in your God box. First of all, how different is what you believe today from what you learned as a child? We go from basic math to advanced math. We learn to read simple sentences and progress to more complex sentences and words. Most aspects of any subject starts us at a beginner's level, and we progress to more complex levels. The same principle seems to hold true for almost everything in our lives but religious thought and belief. Most people I encounter hold much the same beliefs and concepts as an adult as they did as a child. It is no wonder some have tossed religion out the door. Their growth in religious thought did not keep up with their growth in other areas.

Now for a second question. When you get involved in a new endeavor, do you enjoy ideas and concepts that make you stretch, or do you want to stay at the ground level where you feel more secure? Apply that to religion. Are you interested in concepts that make you think and stretch your faith or do you like to stay in the safe area of "this is what I've always been told and it is good enough for me"? Watch this last question; it could throw you for a loop. If you found out there was no God, and no hereafter, would you continue to live the way you do now or make some changes? This has particular significance to anyone who faithfully practices the Christian faith. If your answer is that you would make some changes, what would they be? Would you decide you were wasting your time with religion? If so, you have just placed yourself in the majority group who are Christian in order to secure a heavenly reward.

When it comes to religious belief and practice, there are several things of importance. Religion must be approached with an open mind and intellectual honesty. That seems very difficult for many people to do. It is especially difficult for some raised in fundamentalist approaches to religion. They approach religion with a closed mind to any new idea. I view this as being controlled by their religion. Again, that can be in any denomination or any religion. Some have no difficulty at all in approaching religious thoughts or ideas. They have a different type of closed mind. They just throw out the whole thing. Believe it or not, religion is controlling them in a subtly different manner. Control can be manifested in what we reject, as well as in what we accept.

Religious practice is best experienced in the building of a fellowship, community, or gathering based upon mutual concerns, and love and acceptance of each other. It should also reach beyond its own group with outreach to others. Not an outreach based on desire to convert, but based on a desire to help those in need. Resentment and ostracism would not be a part of such a religious practice. This means disagreement would be seen as an opportunity to grow and serve rather than an opportunity to feel offended and take your marbles and go home. It would be a group in which values and behaviors are more valued than particular beliefs, doctrines, or creeds. I like the words of St. Francis of Assisi when he said, "Preach the gospel at all times. Use words if necessary." This simply translates to what you do being more important than what you say. An old saying comes to mind: "What he is doing speaks so loud I can't hear what he is saying." Some words of Mahatma Gandhi also seem appropriate here. "I would have been a Christian had it not been for Christians." He also said, "I like your Christ. I do not like your Christians. They are so unlike your Christ." I point to the two great commandments Jesus put in simple words. They are: love God and love your neighbor. This was reinforced by Paul in Romans 13:9 when he wrote, "*...and any other commandment, are summed up in this word, 'Love your neighbor as yourself.'*" 1 John 4:7 sums it up very nicely: *"Beloved, let us love one another, because love is from God, everyone who loves is born of God and loves God."* These two verses speak to me of action, not "correct beliefs"! Being a part of a community like this is being involved in the true purpose of the Christian religion. I maintain the purpose of religion is not to control but to live out the command to love!

I am sometimes asked about the word "love." The word certainly is well-known in our culture. We readily proclaim our love to all things, from the inanimate to people. For my use here, the best answer I can give is contained in another scripture. I may be accused of quoting so much scripture I am proof-texting. Fundamentalists like proof-texting so they should not complain about my use of scripture. It is 1 Corinthians 13:4-8a,"*Love is patient; love is kind, love is not envious or boastful or arrogant or rude. It does not insist on its own way; it is not irritable or resentful; it does rejoice in wrong-doing, but rejoices in truth. It bears all things, believes all things, hopes all things, endures all things. Love never ends.*" A short personal exercise is necessary to get a strong interpretation of these verses. Wherever the word "love" or the pronoun "it" appears, replace them with your own name and read the verses. No need to ask what is asked about so much of scripture, "Did it really happen?" The question to ask here when you use your own name is, "Does it happen?" I don't believe any of the words make a demand for "correct beliefs." I think they do say a lot about correct actions. As we struggle with how well we practice love in our own lives, I like the words of a prayer I found with no author listed, just titled, "Prayer of a Dead Slave": "Oh Lord, I ain't what I wanta be. Oh Lord, I ain't what I oughta be—and Oh Lord, I ain't what I'm gonna be. But thanks Lord, I ain't what I used to be!—AMEN"

Keep in mind that none of us have all the answers. The way we see things may not be—change that—is not the way it is. Be willing to listen to others—you might learn something. Too often we are guilty of searching our minds for an answer before we understand the question. This is not to say everything you have been taught and believe should be scrapped. It does mean you need to be conscious that what you have had in your God box since childhood may not express the truth, the whole truth, and nothing but the truth. If we were able to define God and how God works, God would not be God.

I close this chapter with a quote by Karen Armstrong from her book *The Great Transformation*. "The test is simple; if people's beliefs—secular or religious—make them belligerent, intolerant, and unkind about other people's faith, they are not 'skillful.' If, however, their convictions impel them to act compassionately and to honor the stranger,

RELIGION: HOW? WHY?

then they are good, helpful and sound." She goes on to say that in any major faith tradition, this should be what describes true religiosity. I would add I believe what Karen Armstrong describes is true religiosity combined with true spirituality. Are you religious, spiritual, or both? You decide.

CONCLUSION

Let's suppose we could place some readers into a room. Think in terms of a jury and make it twelve. Maybe you would be one of them. The jury's task is to agree on what beliefs should go into a God box. Is the Bible the word of God or God's words? Who or what is the God in which you believe? What was the mission of Jesus on Earth? Are there miracles, and if so, are they the work of God? Is there a hereafter, and if so, what is it like? You can already see I have set an impossible task. What we are doing is messing with everyone's God box.

Some additional guidelines may help in reaching a decision. If some evidence does not support a conclusion, it is not a valid conclusion. For this task, faith alone cannot substitute for all other supporting material. Words of credible scholars are acceptable. Remember what I said about credible scholars? They work with the materials on hand and see what conclusions they arrive at from the research. They do not decide in advance the conclusion they want to reach and slant the research accordingly. Another thing that can't be used is, "But it has always been this way!" Even with this additional information, I have little doubt but what we would have here is a hung jury.

Maybe we should task the jury to come up with one issue on which they could agree. We may get some kind of watered-down verdict. The hard issues would remain untouched. The task first assigned to the jury

CONCLUSION

has still not been accomplished.

We dismiss the jury and let any person interested be a one-person judge seeking answers to the questions presented to the jury. How many judges will we have? What happens when we bring them all together? We will have pandemonium and still no unanimous verdict.

We find out is it difficult to arrive at answers to questions about religious beliefs on which agreement can be reached. We have different denominations and different major faith groups because people do see things differently. That can be good. Whatever method is used, I believe it is in seeking answers we discover new truth. Maybe in sharing information, you come to the realization your God box needs refurbished. That is a good thing.

In real life, each person is a judge of how the questions raised in this book are answered. I stated early in the book, I do not have all the answers. I stated I sometimes like to create questions. I repeat, it is in asking the questions that we have the opportunity of discovering new truth. If you are more interested in security than in truth, you aren't going to touch the questions. You already have your "correct beliefs" in your God box. You have the lid on tight. Convince me there is no fear factor in your decision.

Only one thing remains. The book is finished. I have given my view on a number of issues. I have written about issues where I disagree with fundamentalists. I hope I have raised pertinent questions. Now for one last thought. I can't tell you how to do it, but what's in your God box? You decide!

BIBLIOGRAPHY

Alexander, Eben, M.D. *Proof of Heaven*. New York: Simon & Schuster Paperbacks, 2012.

Armstrong, Karen, *The Battle for God*. New York: The Random House Publishing Group, 2000.
_____. *The Great Transformation*. New York: Alfred A. Knopf, 2006.
_____. *A History of God*. New York: Ballantine Books, 1993.
_____. *In the Beginning*. New York: Ballantine Books, 1996.
_____. *A Short History of Myth*. New York: Canongate, 2005.

Bass, Diana Butler, *Christianity After Religion*. New York: Harper One, 2012.

Bell, Rob, *Love Wins: A Book About Heaven, Hell, and the Fate of Every Person Who Ever Lived*. New York: Harper One, 2011.

Beutner, Edward F., ed., *Listening to the Parables of Jesus*. Santa Rosa, California: Polebridge Press, 2007.

Blaker, Kimberly, ed., *The Fundamentals of Extremism*. New Boston,

BIBLIOGRAPHY

Michigan: New Boston Books, Inc.

Bonhoeffer, Dietrich, *Creation and Fall: Temptation*. New York: Harper & Row, 1959.

Borg, Marcus J., *The God We Never Knew*. San Francisco: HarperCollins, 1998.
_____. *The Heart of Christianity*. San Francisco: HarperCollins, 2003.
_____. *Jesus*. San Francisco: HarperCollins, 2006.
_____. *Meeting Jesus Again for the First Time*. San Francisco: HarperCollins, 1995.
_____. *Reading the Bible Again for the First Time*. San Francisco: HarperCollins, 2002.
_____. *Speaking Christian*. New York: Harper One, 2011.

Borg, Marcus J., and Crossan, John Dominic, *The First Christmas*. New York: HarperCollins, 2007.
_____. *The First Paul*. New York: HarperCollins, 2009.
_____. *The Last Week*. San Francisco, CA: Harper San Francisco, 2006.

Borg, Marcus J., & Wright, N. T., *The Meaning of Jesus*. San Francisco: HarperCollins, 2000.

Brenneman, Richard J., *Deadly Blessings: Faith Healings on Trial*. Buffalo, New York: Prometheus Books, 1990.

Brown, Delwin, *What Does a Progressive Christian Believe?* New York: Church Publishing Incorporated, 2008.

Burns, Elizabeth, *The Late Liz*. New York: Popular Library, 1961.

Campolo, Tony, *Is Jesus a Republican or a Democrat?* Dallas Texas:

Word Publishing, 1995.

Chopra, Deepak, *Life After Death.* New York: Three Rivers Press, 2006.

Cousins, Norman, *The Celebration of Life—A Dialogue on Immortality and Infinity.* New York: Harper & Row, Publishers, 1974.

Crossan, John Dominic, *God & Empire.* San Francisco: HarperCollins, 2007.
_____. *Who Killed Jesus?* San Francisco: HarperCollins, 1996.

Crossan, John Dominic & Watts, Richard G., *Who is Jesus?* Louisville: Westminster John Knox Press, 1996.

Cullman, *Immortality of the Soul or Resurrection of the Dead?* New York: The Macmillan Co., 1958.

Dawkins, Richard, *The God Delusion.* Great Britain: Bantam Press, 2006.

de Chardin, Teilhard, *Christianity and Evolution.* Translated by Rene Hague. London: William Collins Sons & Co Ltd., 1969.

Dennett, Daniel C., *Breaking the Spell: Religion as a Natural Phenomenon.* New York: Penguin Books, 2006.

D'Souza, Dinesh, *What's So Great About Christianity?* Washington, DC: Regnery Publishing, Inc., 2007.

Edward, John, *Crossing Over.* San Diego, California: Jodere Group, Inc, 2001.
_____. *One Last Time.* New York: The Berkley Publishing Group, 1998.

BIBLIOGRAPHY

Edwards, Paul, *Reincarnation: A critical Examination.* Amherst, New York: Prometheus Books, 1996.

Ehrman, Bart D., *Forged.* New York: HarperCollins, 2011.
_____. *God's Problem.* New York: HarperCollins, 2008.
_____. *Jesus: Apocalyptic Prophet of the New Millennium.* New York: Oxford University Press, 1999.
_____. *Jesus, Interrupted.* New York: HarperCollins, 2009.
_____. *Lost Christianities.* New York: Oxford University Press, 2003.
_____. *Lost Scriptures.* New York: Oxford University Press, 2003.
_____. *Misquoting Jesus.* New York: HarperCollins, 2005.
_____. *Peter, Paul, & Mary Magdalene.* New York: Oxford University Press, 2006.

Elnes, Eric, *The Phoenix Affirmations: A New Vision for the Future of Christianity.* San Francisco, CA, Jossey-Bass, 2006.

Ewen, Pamela Binnings, *Faith on Trial.* Nashville, TN: Broadman and Holman Publishers, 1999.

Fosdick, Harry Emerson, *A Guide to Understanding the Bible.* New York: Harper & Brothers Publishers, 1956.

Frankl, Viktor E., *The Unconscious God.* New York: Simon & Schuster, 1975.

Garlow, James L. and Wall, Keith, *Heaven and the Afterlife.* Grand Rapids, MI: Bethany House Publishers, 2009.

Geering, Lloyd, *Christianity without God.* Santa Rosa, California: Polebridge Press, 2002.

Godsey, R. Kirby, *Is God a Christian?* Macon, Georgia: Mercer University Press, 2011.

_____. *When We Talk About God…Let's Be Honest.* Macon, Georgia: Mercer University Press, 2006.

Gomes, Peter J., *The Good Book.* New York: William Morrow and Company, Inc., 1996.

Gonzalez-Wippler, Migene, *What Happens After Death?* St. Paul, Minnesota: Llewellyn Publications, 1997.

Harris, Sam, *Letter to a Christian Nation.* New York: Alfred A. Knopf, 2006.

Hitchens, Christopher, *God Is Not Great.* New York: Hachette Book Group USA, 2007.

James, Eric, *A Life of Bishop John A. T. Robinson.* Grand Rapids, MI: William B. Erdmans Publishing Co, 1987.

James, William, *The Varieties of Religious Experience.* New York: Collier Books, 1961.

Jeeves, Malcolm A. & Berry, R. J., *Science, Life, and Christian Belief.* Grand Rapids, MI: Baker Books, 1998.

Jones, Timothy Paul, *Misquoting Truth.* Downers Grove, IL: InterVarsity Press, 2007.

Keen, Sam, *Hymns to an Unknown God.* New York: Bantam Books, 1994.

Killinger, John, *Leave It to the Spirit.* New York: Harper & Row, Publishers, 1971.

BIBLIOGRAPHY

_____. *Ten Things I Learned Wrong from a Conservative Church.* New York: The Crossroad Publishing Company, 2002.

Kirsch, Jonathan, *The Harlot by the Side of the Road.* New York: Ballantine Books, 1997.

Komoszewski, J. Ed; Sawyer, M. James and Wallace, Daniel B., *Reinventing Jesus.* Grand Rapids, MI: Kregel Publications, 2006.

LaGrand, Louis E., PhD, *Messages and Miracles.* St. Paul, Minnesota: Llewellyn Publications, 1999.

Langley, Noel, *Edgar Cayce on Reincarnation.* New York: Warner Books, Inc. 1967.

Loftus, John W., *Why I Became an Atheist.* Amherst, NY: Prometheus Books, 2008.

Ludemann, Gerd, *Heretics.* London: SCM Press Ltd., 1996.
_____. *Virgin Birth? The Real Story of Mary and Her Son Jesus.* Harrisburg, PA: Trinity Press International, 1998.

Martin, Stephen Hawley, *The Science of Life After Death.* Richmond, VA: The Oaklea Press, 2009.

McLennan, Rev. Scotty, *Jesus Was a Liberal.* New York: Palgrave Macmillan, 2009.

McNeill, John T., *Makers of the Christian Tradition.* New York: Harper & Row, 1964.

Messadie, Gerald, *A history of the Devil.* New York: Kodansha International, 1996.

Meyers, Robin R., *Saving Jesus from the Church*. New York: Harper One, 2009.

Mills, David, *Atheist Universe: The Thinking Person's Answer to Christian Fundamentalism*. Berkeley, CA: Ulysses Press, 2006.

Moody, Raymond A., Jr., M.D., *Life After Life*. New York: Bantam Books, 1975.

Pagels, Elaine, *Adam, Eve, and the Serpent*. New York: Vintage Books, 1989.
_____. *The Gnostic Gospels*. New York: Random House, Inc., 1979.
_____. *The Origin of Satan*. New York: Vintage Books, 1996.
_____. *Revelations, Visions, Prophecy, & Politics in the Book of Revelation*. New York: Penguin Group, 2012.

Pagels, Elaine, and King, Karen L., *Reading Judas*. New York: Penguin Group, 2007.

Polkinghorne, John, *Faith, Science & Understanding*. New Haven: Yale University Press, 2000.
_____. *The God of Hope and the End of the World*. New Haven: Yale University Press, 2002.

Powelson, Mark, and Riegert, Ray, editors, *The Lost Gospel Q*. Berkeley, CA: Ulysses Press, 1996.

Randy, James, *The Faith Healers*. Buffalo, NY: Prometheus Press, 1987.

Rawlings, Maurice S., MD, *To Hell and Back*. Nashville: Thomas Nelson Publishers, 1993.

BIBLIOGRAPHY

Riley, Gregory J., *The River of God.* San Francisco: HarperCollins, 2001.

Robinson, John A. T., *Honest to God.* Philadelphia: The Westminster Press, 1963.
_____. *In the End God.* New York: Harper and Row, 1968.
_____. *Jesus and His Coming.* Nashville: Abington Press, 1957.

Russell, Jeffrey Burton, *A History of Heaven.* Princeton, NJ: Princeton University Press, 1997.

Sanford, Charles B., *The Religious Life of Thomas Jefferson.* Charlottesville, Virginia: University Press of Virginia, 1988.

Scott, Bernard Brandon, *Jesus Reconsidered.* Santa Rosa, CA: Polebridge Press, 2007.

Schwartzentruber, Michael, Editor, *The Emerging Christian Way.* Kelowna, BC, Canada: CopperHouse, 2006.

Scott, Bernard Brandon, *Jesus Reconsidered.* Santa Rosa, California: Polebridge Press, 2007.
_____. *The Trouble with Resurrection.* Salem, Oregon: Polebridge Press, 2010.

Sheryl, Greg, *A Christian Minister Responds to Bart Ehrman.* Lexington, KY, 2010.

Smith, Huston, *The Soul of Christianity.* San Francisco, CA: Harper San Francisco, 2005.
_____. *Why Religion Matters.* New York: HarperCollins Publisher Inc., 2001.

Spong, John Shelby, *Born of a Woman.* San Francisco: HarperCollins, 1992.

_____. *A New Christianity for a New World.* San Francisco: HarperCollins, 2001.
_____. *Eternal Life: A New Vision.* New York: Harper One, 2009.
_____. *Here I Stand.* San Francisco: HarperCollins, 2000.
_____. *Jesus for the Nonreligious.* San Francisco: HarperCollins, 2007.
_____. *Liberating the Gospels.* San Francisco: HarperCollins, 1996.
_____. *Re-claiming the Bible for a Non-Religious World.* New York: Harper One, 2011.
_____. *Rescuing the Bible from Fundamentalism.* San Francisco: HarperCollins, 1991.
_____. *Resurrection: Myth or Reality?* San Francisco: HarperCollins, 1994.
_____. *The Sins of Scripture.* San Francisco: HarperCollins, 2005.
_____. *This Hebrew Lord.* San Francisco: HarperCollins, 1993.
_____. *Why Christianity Must Change or Die.* San Francisco: HarperCollins, 1999.

St. Clair, David, *Psychic Healers.* Garden City, New York: Doubleday & Company, Inc., 1974.

Tickle, Phyllis, *The Great Emergence.* Grand Rapids, Michigan: Baker Books, 2008.

Tillich, Paul, *Dynamics of Faith.* New York: Harper & Brothers, 1957.
_____. *The New Being.* New York: Charles Scribner's Sons, 1955.

Weatherhead, Leslie D., *The Christian Agnostic.* Nashville: Abington, 1965.

BIBLIOGRAPHY

Weil, Andrew, M.D., *Spontaneous Healing.* New York: Alfred A. Knopf, Inc., 1995.

White, Mel, *Religion Gone Bad.* New York: Penguin Group, 2006.

Wright, N. T., *Surprised by Hope.* New York: HarperCollins, 2008.

Yancey, Philip, *Prayer: Does It Make a Difference?* Grand Rapids, Michigan: Zondervan, 2006.

Young, Alan, *Spiritual Healings--Miracle or Mirage?* Marina del Rey, California: DeVorss & Company, 1981.

York, Tripp, *The Devil Wears Nada.* Eugene, Oregon: Cascade Books, 2011.

Zukav, Gary, *Soul Stories.* New York: Fireside, 2000.
_____. *The Seat of the Soul,* New York: Fireside, 1989.

Lightning Source UK Ltd.
Milton Keynes UK
UKOW02f1012041215

264032UK00001B/42/P